Telling the Bees

Telling the Bees

Barbara Fowler

HHG
HILLHELEN
Group Publishers LLC

Editor's note: In *Telling the Bees*, author Barbara Fowler uses fictitious
names referring to doctors, patients, and families to protect their
privacy. Place names, events, and celebrities are actual nonfiction.

Library of Congress Cataloging-in-Publication Data
ISBN: 979-8-9896268-8-5

Printed and bound in the United States of America by Ingram
Lightning Source

Edited by Jacque Hillman and Katie Gould
Layout and design by Katie Gould
Cover art by Wanda Stanfill
Chapter art by Wanda Stanfill

The HillHelen Group LLC
470 North Parkway, Suite C
Jackson, TN 38305

The HillHelen Group LLC
1761 West Stanton Avenue
Apache Junction, AZ 85120

(731) 394-2894
www.hillhelengrouppublishers.com
hillhelengroup@gmail.com

Dedication

For my four Bs:
Brian, Benjamin Z.,
Bradley Z., and Barrymore Z.

Acknowledgments

The pitfall of having an acknowledgments page is that you inevitably leave someone out who ought to be thanked. I have many people to thank for their help over the years, but for this writing, I am concentrating on only a few.

Among the people to thank for helping me get this memoir into print are Bill and Julia Kipp. Julia suggested that I go to Dr. Hal Poe's C. S. Lewis seminar retreat at Montreat in North Carolina. At the end of the sessions, Dr. Poe always includes an *Inklings* hour. During that time, authors read their latest writings and get responses from the audience comprised mainly of professors, pastors, college students, and those interested in Lewis.

I asked Dr. Poe if it would be appropriate for me to read a chapter of my memoir even though it had nothing to do with Lewis. He was very kind to include me on the roster.

Once it was determined that I could get feedback from people who did not know me, Bill and Julia; Brian, my husband; and Barry, my son, made the trek to Montreat. John White, pastor of First Presbyterian Church, offered us his cabin in Montreat so that we would have a place to stay while attending the seminar. Thank you.

Not only did Bill and Julia drive us, but they helped rework some of my writing and willingly sat through several readings of the chapter with me.

Thanks to all who attended the seminar, for they spurred me to finish my memoir. Before I read my chapter, I asked the educated audience to please give me constructive criticism at the end. I explained that their impartial commentary would be invaluable.

After I read the chapter, I expected lots of advice and suggestions; however, what met me was silence. I was ready to be embarrassed, but instead the audience turned out to be so receptive that I was astounded. One audience member asked about Barry. When I told them he was sitting in the front row, they all applauded. I was shocked.

The person who really put me on the path to finishing my memoir was Dr. Poe. He offered to edit my work and get it publishing-ready. Thank you for your offer, reading my work, and writing a blurb for this book.

I came home from Montreat in high spirits and announced to my family that I was not to be disturbed until I finished this tome. Don't ask for food or where something is! I thank Brian, Ben, and Barry for fending for themselves while I wrote long into the nights.

I thank Kevin Jerge for agreeing to read my memoir and meet with me to discuss the next steps. Since he had written a memoir of his youth, I knew he could give me important information. We had discussed getting an agent and how difficult it was to get in the door. He, too, had difficulty finding an agent and decided to self-publish. He asked me an important question: What do you want to do with this memoir? I said I wanted to leave something behind that ensured we would not be forgotten. He suggested I should self-publish.

Since I knew several people who worked with Jacque Hillman, I decided to call her. This phone call put my goal into motion. Thank you for your willingness to publish my memoir.

I also wish to thank Molly Coffman, my former colleague, friend, and reading partner for reading the memoir and writing a blurb.

Finally, thank you to Bruce and Mary Ann Hamblen for reading my work, for encouraging me, and for their forty-year friendship with me.

High praise for *Telling the Bees*

"Barbara Fowler bares her soul with a narrative that weaves through the pain and resilience as her family navigates profound loss and unexpected healing. *Telling the Bees* captures the essence of human endurance, blending inspirational folklore with life's raw truths. Fowler's storytelling is both a lament and a celebration of the human spirit, reminding us of the beauty that can emerge from the depths of sorrow. I am grateful I read her poignant memoir. A must-read for anyone seeking meaning amidst life's unpredictability."

—**Kevin Jerge,** author of *Go to Your Happy Place* and a member of First Presbyterian Church, Jackson, Tennessee

"Barbara Fowler has given us a story of tragedy and resilience, of despair and hope, of loss and faith. She has experienced the worst that life can offer, and she has found grace and comfort in the midst of death. Her book offers encouragement and the comfort of consolation to all of us."

—**Dr. Harry Lee Poe,** author of *Becoming C. S. Lewis, The Making of C. S. Lewis,* and *The Completion of C. S. Lewis*

"In this moving story about a journey through unimaginable, unexplainable heartbreak, Barbara writes with courage and tenderness, with bold faith and honest doubt. Her faith—forged through fire—is not polished, but it is uncommon. In a world quick to offer neat answers or to explain away suffering, this memoir offers something rarer: the sacredness of simply holding on."

—**Dr. Molly Coffman,** Madison Academic Magnet High School, Jackson, Tennessee

"This memoir is a story, a story of life. A story of brokenness and a story of healing. A story of despair and a story of hope. A story of doubt and a story of faith. Barbara Fowler has skillfully woven together these diverse elements to create a passionate and evocative narrative that recounts her family's journey through both heartbreak and exhilaration. This book will captivate you as it leads you through the depths of grief and the heights of joy with all the speed and twists of a roller-coaster. Your heart will be touched, and your mind will be challenged as you read this chronicle of the Fowler family."

—**John White,** pastor, First Presbyterian Church, Jackson, Tennessee

Why *Telling the Bees*?

I first heard of the practice of "telling the bees" from a friend who told me of the Celtic myth in which a bee signified the soul leaving the body. Intrigued by this tradition, I discovered that in the eighteenth and nineteenth centuries in the United States and Europe, it was common to drape a piece of black crepe or black cloth over the beehives of a home when someone in the house has died, indicating that the house was in mourning. It was also the eldest male's duty to inform the bees.

John Greenleaf Whittier's 1858 poem, "Telling the Bees," describes the narrator of the poem returning to his lover's home only to find that his lover has died. The chore-girl in the poem sings to the hives: "Stay at home, pretty bees, fly not hence!/Mistress Mary is dead and gone!" The narrator and the chore-girl note the importance of communicating with the bees so they can all grieve.

Other variations of "telling the bees" that someone has died have been catalogued. For example, Tammy Horn, scholar and apiarist, writes about "ricking." This ritual requires the eldest male of the family to move the beehives to signify that a change has occurred in the family. Another example from F. G. Jenyns's book, *A Book About Bees* (1886), tells that the bees must be alerted of a death at midnight.

Finally, bees seem to have a direct connection to the gods who view their honey as nectar. Artist Akseli Gallen-Kallela depicts the mother of hero Lemminkäinen looking for the bee from the gods that will deliver life-giving nectar to bring her son to life again. Unfortunately, we will never know if the life-giving elixir comes.

When I walk around in my gardens and see bees dipping into the centers of my daylilies' blooms, I tell them to bring me that life-giving ambrosia from the gods. I'm waiting.

Table of Contents

Section 4

Introduction

Telling the Bees

Coming to the South, complete with cotton fields—with a Bible Belt that cinches the girth of Tennessee's 500 miles, with heat and humidity that rival hell's, with citizens whose names are simply initials like JR or TJ or double names like Mary Louise or Billy Bob—was a move that Fate determined was for us.

Our neighbor to the right introduced us to water moccasins by shooting one from his back porch with the biggest shotgun I ever saw. Years of living in various New York locales never scared me as much as when Sam appeared on my back porch with a black moccasin dangling from a rake, announcing that we needed to keep an eye out for these rascals. His grin indicated that he found extreme pleasure in showing this Yankee a thing or two. I huddled my boys around my skirt, protecting them from the evil, headless reptile and the equally evil grin on Sam's face.

That same day, my neighbor to the left came to my back door, offering a tuna casserole and biscuits as a welcome to the neighborhood. Martha, a stern woman with battleship-gray hair, looked us over, gave us a contrived smile, and announced that she had little to do with the neighbors. With that, she refused my offer to come inside and indicated that she would appreciate it if I could return the casserole dish by the end of the week. I thanked her and assured her that the dish would be back in her possession by week's end. She marched off over the lawn, and I didn't see her again until I returned the dish.

Her husband, Joe, on the other hand, seemed to be a meek man who spent his days on their corner lot fussing with the lawn and flowerbeds and frequently stopped his activity to wave with a gloved hand at cars passing by. He seemed not to care if he knew the driver; he simply waved because that is what you do in the South. It was neighborly. Unlike his bride, Joe always spoke and took time to ask about our welfare. His overly friendly demeanor was a definite decision on his part to make up for Martha's surly countenance. Later, I learned the life story of Martha and Joe that explained much of their behaviors.

Brian, Ben, Brad, and I decided to spend only two years in this "cotton field" until we moved on to better parts. In those early years, I did not see the beauty in West Tennessee, nor did I appreciate small-town USA. Madison County was dry, which meant package stores and brown bags when you went out to eat. We were located in a black-white area of the country where not much was tolerated, especially foreigners from the North. Forty years later, the cotton fields are still growing cotton; Madison County is no longer dry; and many people are not racist but many others still are. There is beauty that resides in the suffering of the people and their willingness to endure.

We carried on with our lives, taking so much for granted. School, work, and play occupied our time. I watched my boys play baseball while I graded papers on the bleachers. Every now and then, a cold spell would interrupt the sweltering summers and falls. I complained to my bleacher-sitting moms, "Where are the hot flashes when you need them?"

They snickered but with reserve. In those days, a lady would not refer to private matters so vocally. Around that time, I was told that I was "too direct" to suit them. It was unnecessary.

The next question that would always arise after someone would get to know us was, "Where do y'all go to church?"

We had not considered joining a church, but Brian thought we ought to be Presbyterians because he attended that denomination as a child. Since the boys should have church training, we joined First Presbyterian Church on Highland Avenue in Jackson, Tennessee. The church and its grounds appealed to our sense of tradition. It remains the prettiest church complex in Jackson. The people who comprise the congregation—including the Baxters, Grangers, and Lamberts—are also steeped in Jackson's history and traditions. The members, all upstanding citizens of Jackson, did not overwhelm us. There were no home visits or people checking on us if we did not show up one Sunday. I appreciated that; after all, we knew what we were doing.

In retrospect, the decision to join First Presbyterian was one of the better decisions we made in our lives because the church became the one constant I could count on to assist when we needed it. Although the former statement sounds terribly self-serving, I believe that to be called Christian means to serve above all. Without question, I found the members of First Presbyterian to be good servants, especially when life's detours led to troubling destinations.

By 1989, we were churched, belonged to the Episcopal Day School community where I taught and the boys attended, and became part of the United Foods community in Bells, Tennessee, where Brian worked. I did not realize that these were the "salad days" of our young family's lives. Sending Ben and his friend RJ off with lunch on summer mornings to explore the pond, dam, and ditches behind our house, like Huck and Tom, and telling them to be back by six o'clock or else, seemed so normal. Telling Brad he could only ride to the end of the dead-end street and back without me watching him seemed normal. Watching the boys play baseball at Lion's Field until dusk was sometimes boring but also seemed right. Attending homemade ice cream socials or potluck suppers at church during the long, hot summers seemed quaint but pleasant.

Our lives smacked of a Norman Rockwell painting, one that would continue with many Thanksgivings, Christmases, and birthdays until the arrival of grandchildren and great-grandchildren who would be incorporated into the painting. I never considered that I would be in my own version of an 1897 Akseli Gallen-Kallela painting, sewing my son together and praying to my God to bring the honey that would bring him to life again, whether via a bee, a doctor, or a magic troll.

Our Norman Rockwell painting first changed on September 19, 1985, when I gave birth to our third son, Barrymore Zeb Fowler. He began life prematurely as a five-pound, five-ounce mistake with a mass of curly hair. Initially, he had difficulty thriving, but soon he caught on to the nursing regimen and began to gain weight, much to our relief. We were again on track and would do what we could to raise three reasonably well-adjusted children. Our expectations for the children were simple: Learn, go to college, build a career, get married, have children, and bury your parents. Unfortunately, everything began to unravel with Barry's birth and was never knit together again in quite the same way.

I placed all the photos from 1977 to 2004 in beautiful *Lebkuchen* (gingerbread) boxes that sit on the dry sink with a thick layer of dust protecting the precious memories inside, for I cannot bring myself to even look at the photos without spiraling into the abyss of depression from which I nearly did not escape. Those photos are a recollection of life as it should have been, at least in my mind. If I did everything right, I could control all actions because I was the creator of those actions. Never once did I consider the ball from left field that I could not see coming until it was too late.

When I think of us before 1989, I think green. I think youth. I think of a contrived confidence that we were above the fray; we were invincible, much like a teen who doesn't believe anything bad will ever happen to him because the world is his oyster. When something untoward finally does happen, there is shock, disbelief, and a nightmarish quality to the event. There is the belief that the teen will awaken, believing the event was a nightmare and his unblemished life will continue as before. Only it doesn't.

As I look back on the 1980s and '90s, nothing is clear. The events blur and blend like a dream hopping from image to image that the retiring mind creates without ever giving the dreamer much to remember. However, in May 1989, we awoke to a reality none of us ever dared to dream.

Image courtesy of the Finnish National Gallery

Akseli Gallen-Kallela's 1897 painting, *Lemminkäinen's Mother.*

Chapter 1

Le Bonheur Children's Hospital

To borrow from Charles Dickens: Having children is the best thing that ever happened to me, and the worst. By the time Barry was three, we were working hard to create lives for ourselves and for each other that would reap great benefits in the future. I signed Ben up to take Suzuki violin lessons, Brad to play soccer, and Barry to learn in play school.

By this time, Grandma and Grandpa Fowler had moved to Jackson to be near their only grandchildren. My initial reaction to their move was fraught with apprehension. Grandma was everything I did not want to be. I was, after all, a woman of the 1960s who could do everything well—juggling a career, family, marriage, and friends. The presence of the grandparents would cramp my style, or so I thought. I write this with a great deal of shame because my hubris was over the top. In later years, I made some amends for my haughty behavior, but at that time, I was so caught up in how our lives should play out that I did not want anyone interfering in that plan. I was afraid that Grandpa and Grandma would be that kind of interference.

How immature and selfish my thinking was. Any jealousies that reared their ugly heads in that first year of togetherness were soon dispatched because the need we had for each other was monumental.

Grandpa died in 1986 after several heart attacks, leaving Grandma alone and nearly penniless in a place far away from the home she once knew. We were her only solace while she attempted to navigate through life without her mate of forty-six years. After his death, she was a constant presence in our home, which, like a two-edged sword, presented its own difficulties and conveniences.

By early spring of 1989, Barry began to have asthma attacks. At first, these were not too severe. Then, one Saturday afternoon after we attended a parade in downtown Jackson, his face turned blue, and we hurried him to the nearest convenient care clinic. He was given a breathing treatment, a shot, and a prescription, and he returned to a normal color. The asthma attacks continued for a time but were soon replaced with severe leg pains in the night. During the day, he seemed to be fine.

The cycle of asthma attacks, nightly leg pains, and weight loss were suspicious, but Dr. Finster found no good reason to be alarmed. I brought Barry to his office multiple times, only to be told to give him another round of antibiotics. After three rounds, I insisted that Dr. Finster run some more tests. He was openly annoyed with me but agreed to perform a barium enema that proved absolutely nothing.

Dr. Finster then told me that I was spoiling Barry and that I should stop it immediately. I tried to explain to him that Barry cried bitterly during the night, wailing that his thin little legs hurt. The only way we could calm him was to hold him. Needless to say, after six weeks of little sleep, I was in no mood to be told that I was spoiling my child.

That same week, Barry had another asthma attack that resulted in another convenient care stop. The doctor on duty that night decided to run a blood test on Barry and gave him a breathing treatment. After I told him of the past six weeks of antibiotic treatment, leg pain at night, weight loss, and all-around crankiness, he suggested I go see another doctor, perhaps at Le Bonheur Children's Hospital in Memphis, Tennessee.

The prospect of going to Memphis frightened us. We had, of course, visited Memphis many times for one event or another. Each time we drove past Le Bonheur and St. Jude Children's Research Hospital, I always averted my eyes because I did not want to look at buildings that housed suffering little children. In my mind, if I could keep places like that at arm's length, their tentacles could not reel in my children or me.

Silly as such thinking may be, I don't think it is far wrong. Parents simply do not want to believe that anything horrible could happen to their perfect children. And, of course, for those children and parents who must suffer in such institutions, we have much compassion, but we do not want to know too much. Knowing would make us accountable and responsible to help these unfortunates in some way. Besides the knowing, the discomfort we feel being around people who are hurting so much is simply not something we want to witness. I certainly felt that way.

At Le Bonheur, we saw Dr. Wilson, a diagnostician. She scheduled a number of blood tests and a CT scan. At the end of the morning, Dr. Wilson had not found anything conclusive. She suggested we go home and come back in a few days when she would have other tests ready to run.

Our family was in the eighth week of trying to get to the bottom of Barry's problem, and my nerves were frayed. I could only respond to her suggestion in one way: "Dr. Wilson, if we go home without a definitive answer as to Barry's pain and what we can do about it, we will not return. I am sick and tired of being shuffled to the back when I know my child is sick. Somebody must be able to determine his problem! I will go to the ends of the earth to find someone who cares."

Then I ran out of steam and cried. She studied me and Barry a few minutes, got up without saying a word, and quietly closed the door behind her. I cried into Barry's curly hair. Brian felt uncomfortable, as he often does when I make a horse's ass of myself. Thus, we waited.

Dr. Wilson finally appeared with papers in tow. She said we had been checked into Room 415 and that she would set up the tests she wanted to run on Barry as soon as we signed the papers she spread out in front of us. I signed by the *x*'s, not caring what I was signing, as long as she was going to cure Barry. Relief spread through me like cold water over one's head on a hot day. Somebody listened to me. Somebody heard. She heard my plea.

I blubbered thanks in her direction, but she was gone as soon as the papers were signed. We were whisked to Room 415 to await tests and an answer. Of course, the nights continued to be brutal. Barry's cries pierced me to the core. Initially, the doctor refused to give Barry anything because she did not want to mask any of his symptoms, but later in the week, as she ruled out one disease after another, she gave him and me relief in the form of some medication. I stayed with him 24/7. During the week, phone calls and gifts for Barry kept us connected to home.

By day five of our internment in Room 415, we were told that no more tests were scheduled for the day. I asked the nurse if a treatment plan had been put in place for Barry's disease. She said the doctor would see us shortly and would explain what needed to be done. In the silent room, I could only pray: "Dear God, please help the doctor cure Barry." Surely, there was a shot, a pill, or some sort of treatment that would cure what ailed him. It simply couldn't be that serious, but my hands were sweating, and I noticed a slightly louder beat of my heart in my ears.

As the door to Room 415 opened, five people in white coats filed in and stood around the bed in a semicircle. Dr. Wilson carried a clipboard. The young, blonde Dr. Anderson, who carried out Dr. Wilson's orders, and three others watched us. At that moment, time slowed, speech slowed, and my comprehension came to a complete halt. Dr. Wilson said things that to this day are a jumble of rumbles. I could pick out a few words: "home . . . weekend . . . St. Jude . . . Monday . . . 8 a.m. . . . go home today." At the end of her speech, I heard her say, "Questions." Did I have any questions?

My mind whirled. *You have to be kidding me! Why do we have to be at St. Jude on Monday at eight? Seriously, cancer! Barry's only three! What? Neur- . . . What kind of cancer? You've made this up! Dr. Garcia. Never heard of him. Cancer. Brian, tell them they're wrong. You've got to run more tests. Second opinion.*

Dr. Wilson and the three other white coats left. Only young, blonde, blue-eyed Dr. Anderson stayed. She picked up Barry and walked the halls with him while Brian and I attempted to wrap our minds around the concept that our son had a rare cancer. I looked at Brian as though he was a stranger in this nightmare. Why wasn't he saying anything? Why wasn't he coming up with a solution? Who was he?

Barry's father and mother should have known what to do, but they didn't. We were at sea hanging on to whatever lifesaving device we could think of to keep from drowning in our sorrow. Wasn't this the time to rally around Barry? He was the one who was sick. No, we were all sick, all dying. This news could not be real. Still, we said nothing.

The same door to Room 415 opened again with Dr. Anderson and Barry holding a teddy bear in the doorway. "We're back from visiting everybody, and Barry is ready to go home for the weekend," the doctor said.

Their appearance jolted us out of our private reverie. As is usually the case with me, I do better when I'm given an assignment, such as "pack your clothes and go home for the weekend." Dr. Anderson stayed with us as we packed the cards and gifts into our suitcase, and she reiterated much of what Dr. Wilson had said on that fateful morning.

The cancer was called neuroblastoma. Dr. Garcia would be Barry's primary physician. He would be in the most capable hands in the world. St. Jude Children's Research Hospital is the premier hospital for children's cancer in the world. He would be given the best care available.

"Dr. Anderson, you've said nothing about Barry being cured of this cancer," I said.

Her blue eyes shifted away from me, and she offered no answer.

Chapter 2

Arrival at Home

Leaving Le Bonheur Children's Hospital was the easy part; coming home to the expectant faces of the boys, Grandma, and friends was the hard part. On the way home, I held Barry in my lap, sticking my face into his beautiful, curly, brown hair, soft as down. I wanted to remember how that three-year-old hair smelled and felt, for it would soon be gone. His eyes with dark circles looked at me pleadingly to make him feel better. I promised he would feel better soon. Every bit of me was holding my emotions in check because we had to make some big decisions for which we had no guidelines.

"How are we going to tell the boys, Grandma, and our friends that Barry has neuroblastoma, a cancer that will most likely kill him within a year?" I asked Brian without looking at him. We needed a plan.

"I don't know how to tell them other than what we know," he answered in his usual matter-of-fact manner.

I was tempted to gloss over, or sweep under the carpet, the reality we were facing to make it more palatable for the boys, but "re-creating the wheel plan of life" was too difficult for me to conjure. One of us would have to stay home and care for Barry while he was undergoing treatment at St. Jude for however long it would take. I knew the lion's share of the responsibility for his care would be mine. I would have to quit my job at the Episcopal Day School that I loved. Brian would continue to work and give us food and a roof over our heads. Grandma would hold down the fort at home when I had to be at St. Jude with Barry. That was about as far as we got on the ride home.

My worry about the future was interrupted by Barry's joy at seeing a "goully-goul" (three-year-old for "motorcycle"). He was thrilled to see several of them on a trip to somewhere. I rolled down the window for him to hear the *brum-brum* of the engines and to see them better. He leaned his curly little head out of the window and waved at the passing motorcyclists. One of them waved back, which caused Barry to erupt in laughter. He was so happy despite the cursed cancer curled in serpentine fashion around his intestines and organs in his abdomen.

I thought I needed to take on some of his attitude toward the revelation we were given: Enjoy the small things in life and put aside the horrors that lurked in places mostly unknown to me. At that moment, I learned to compartmentalize my emotions. I recognized there were things that needed to be felt or processed immediately and things that could wait.

I also learned that life for others, such as the motorcyclists, continued in its forward pace despite our immediate problems. They were probably going toward some fun destination where they would have a raucous lunch with friends and return home feeling gratified that they had such a wonderful day riding in the sunshine of the earth's grace. Of course, at that time, it never occurred to me that they could have a horrific accident in which three of their friends would be airlifted to the nearest hospital and pronounced dead. The possibility was not in my realm of thinking because I was so concerned about Barry and his imminent death. What would that do to our family, to me? I shuddered and decided to be like Scarlett and deal with that tomorrow.

By the way, putting aside what you can't fix until another time is a pretty good way to handle a tough decision if you can manage it. As we neared Jackson, I could feel my stomach tighten, my teeth grind, and a nagging headache making its way to the front of my head. Ben, Brad, and Grandma were waiting for us in the kitchen. We congregated around the kitchen table for a family pow-wow. Everyone was eager to hear the results of the tests, what neuroblastoma was and, specifically, what we planned to do to help Barry get better.

I explained that neuroblastoma is one of the most formidable childhood cancers. It attacks the sympathetic nervous system that runs along the length of the spine. In Barry's case, the tumor had wrapped itself around the internal organs of his abdomen and the aorta. The cancer had also spread to his bone marrow, so the tumor was categorized as Stage D.

We would be going to St. Jude on Monday at eight in the morning to begin treatment. I could hardly look at the boys and Grandma as I reiterated what I knew about this heinous cancer.

The boys, including Barry, were getting fidgety. They had heard enough and wanted to get back to their play. Barry's brothers took him to the toy box and commenced their usual activities. I finally looked at Grandma. Although she cackled intermittently at my narrative, I saw tears standing in her eyes that belied her seeming mirth. She took it upon herself to start some lunch. The kitchen and preparing food of some sort, especially baking something, were always her go-tos for comfort and solace.

The realization that each of us has his own special go-to place where he feels in control and where he feels at peace is as varied as the people on Earth. Brian, too, felt the need to be alone, so he headed to the garden to dig holes to China. I watched the boys play in their Star Wars, Ninja Turtles, and GI Joe worlds and wondered where my go-to place was. I didn't discover it until much later in life, for which I am grateful.

We hurdled over the initial fear of telling the boys and everyone we knew about Barry's condition quite successfully, I thought. At that point, I wanted time to fast-forward to Monday morning so that we could get on with treatment, doing something constructive for Barry. In wishing for the time to fly, I was forgoing precious time together that could mean so much to us. Being the ever ASAP person that I am, I was not wise enough to allow us to live in the moment.

The only thing I had in mind was that I needed to have a last picture taken of the boys together before Barry died. On Saturday morning, after a fitful night of sleep for all of us, especially Barry, I dressed the boys in whatever clean clothing I could find and piled them into the car.

I had no appointment at Olan Mills, but when I explained that this would be the only time we had before Barry started cancer treatments with subsequent hair loss, they agreed to squeeze us in. To this day, I am so glad that I have that photograph of my boys together before being marred by the life-changing hurt that cancer brings into a family. Ben and Brad's eyes are so innocent looking; even Barry's dark-circled eyes under his mass of curls have the quality of innocence. The boys could not understand what cancer could do to them until much later in their lives, and Barry certainly could not grasp what was about to happen to his body.

Chapter 3

First Day at St. Jude

Our first Monday morning at St. Jude Children's Research Hospital was a whirlwind. We had so much to process, to understand, but mostly to accept. The last was by far the most difficult for me. My stomach was churning and my head was aching as we entered the parking lot of the hospital that I had always avoided and viewed with a skewed eye when we drove by it on Interstate 40, but it was no longer avoidable. I wanted to cry and turn around immediately.

The hospital in 1989 was a far different structure from the pink towers that exist today. The building was star-shaped with a central waiting room and hallways extending from the center. Here, patients waited to be called for weights and measures, tests, scans, chemotherapy, or radiation that were to be performed that day. We were also given lunch tickets and tickets to get snack boxes.

If we had to spend the night, we were given vouchers for one of the nearby hotels. The whole St. Jude operation was remarkable to me, especially as no money, other than insurance, was required to be paid for their services. Even our gas mileage was computed, and we were given a check for the trips to St. Jude. Since our monies were basically cut in half with my leave from school, the fact that St. Jude covered our expenses was truly a godsend.

My reaction to the waiting room was more or less, "Let's get this thing done and go." Unfortunately, my patience was tested time and again because I had to learn to wait. Type A personalities do not wait well. Brian, on the other hand, understood waiting, which kept me calmer than I would have been without him.

We were finally called to weights and measures, where Barry was given the number 11052, his ID at St. Jude. He was weighed, measured, and brought to the blood techs, who were lovingly referred to as "vampires." Maggie, a soft, black woman with kind eyes, took Barry into her arms and told me to stand aside while she dealt with Mr. Barrymore!

Just a minute! You are about to stick my baby! How dare you tell me to stand aside! I thought.

Barry was very happy in Maggie's embrace and ignored my fit. In no time, she took several vials of blood, pasted a cartoon Band-Aid over his stick, gave him a choice of toys and suckers, and provided us with directions to our next stop. Over the year, Barry and Maggie became fast friends, and she made sure that she would be the one to stick Barry at every visit. *This is not going to be so bad,* I thought.

Yet, I had a fleeting thought that would appear in my mind's eye every time I saw a child wearing his numbered bracelet. They were marked; they were identified. No, the number was not tattooed on their forearms, but it might as well have been. They were marked, maybe not for the gas chamber, but for death.

I was not able to erase this macabre thought from my mind;

even to this day when we visit St. Jude, that comparison creeps around in my mind.

Our second stop was to see Dr. Garcia, the foremost physician in the world dealing with neuroblastoma. When I first laid eyes on the man, I thought I was looking at a drug dealer from South America. He wore no white doctor coat but sported a white shirt with the sleeves rolled up over his biceps. He was missing the cigarette pack. His manner was quick with us but gentle with Barry. In the small consultation room, Brian and I stood on one side of the gurney on which Barry lay, and Dr. Garcia was on the other side. As he began prodding around Barry's abdomen, Barry began to squirm and cry out.

I was about to stop his probing when he looked up at me over his black-rimmed glasses with piercing, coal-black eyes and said, "Mrs. Fowler, let's get one thing straight. I am the doctor, Barry is the patient, and you are the parent. I think we'll keep it that way." This was not his first rodeo with a noncompliant parent!

Over the year, Dr. Garcia and I developed a kind of relationship that bordered on friendship. We even spoke to groups together to raise money for St. Jude. I would tell the human side of the treatment, and he would explain the scientific side.

I understood, though, that he had to protect himself from getting too close to families because the outcome of the treatment would not always be positive. I asked him and others how they are able to come to St. Jude daily and work with such sick children and their often overbearing and sometimes uncaring parents. All, without fail, said they spent some time on a couch with a psychiatrist or with their religious mentor.

Dr. Garcia was straightforward and told us that Barry would most likely not survive neuroblastoma. Since he was already in Stage D, his chances were slim. Basically, the doctor told us to prepare for a funeral.

Once again, I could not compute what he was saying. Even after chemo, surgery, radiation, and other treatments in this medical Disneyland, he could not promise a good result.

No. Absolutely not. I will not hear anyone talk like this. Barry is my child. He will not die. God will not let him die. I am certain. Dr. Garcia had probably heard this before and more. He promised to do everything in his power and said that we would have to work with him. With that last order, we were sent to the chemo room (aka the Beauty Parlor, but no one is getting his hair done).

A young nurse took our papers and gave us a seat in what looked to me like a La-Z-Boy lounger. Several IV poles attached to the chairs provided hooks upon which the dreaded chemo, blood, plasma, saline, or antibiotics hung to be administered into the ports on the tiny chests of the patients.

At this point, Barry had no port, but he was scheduled to have surgery after his first chemo treatment. The ports saved the children from getting stuck every time blood or some infusion was needed. The problem with the ports was the twenty-step cleaning process that took place at least twice daily to prevent infection.

On the walls around the room, televisions showed cartoons, Oprah, the weather, and various other programs. The room was a hub of activity: nurses flitting from chair to chair; children vomiting into kidney-shaped receptacles; mothers exchanging recipes; laughter; snoozing; eating. The vibe in the room was genial with little sense of the horror evident.

We were ushered to a chair next to a pregnant woman and her bald two-year-old. After we settled in, the small boy offered Barry some of his Cheerios and banana. His offer concluded with said Cheerios and bananas spewing out of his mouth onto the plate. I was horrified, but his mother calmly wiped his mouth and produced clean Cheerios for Barry. I stupidly told Barry not to take any because he might catch something dreadful!

Within a week, Barry was the boy offering food to someone while he was throwing up, and I was the mother wiping him nonchalantly. The whole scene in the Beauty Parlor was surreal.

As a side note, that small boy who offered the Cheerios died within a few months. I spoke with his pregnant mom shortly after his death. She claimed that it was God's will but that He had given her another child. I was left speechless! A replacement child? This was God's will? No, that was unacceptable to me.

When the first day came to a close, we spent the night at the Crowne Plaza. We did not realize how emotionally exhausted we all were until we hit the bed. We would be back at eight the next morning for bone scans, MRIs, CT scans, and other tests. As I lay in bed next to Barry, with Brian in the other bed, I wondered how much of this we could take.

Chapter 4

Prayer

In the St. Jude waiting room in 1989, we parents awaited the next chemical "ride" our children would get on to see how sick they could get. The heart of the building was the place where we waited for doctors to call us; waited, like spiders, to snatch one of the doctors or nurses as they passed from one wing to the other; waited to hear of so-and-so's latest problems; and waited to hear if we could go home.

In the waiting room, we also met each other—all of us who had to watch our children undergo unspeakable treatments. We were careful not to get too close to one another because we did not want to love another child and have to attend his or her funeral. We did not want to know too much about each other because that would open the doors to our lives.

I especially kept to myself because it broke my heart daily to watch the bald children play or lethargically lie on their mothers' laps. I did not want to know them or anything about their likes or dislikes, their experiences, their treatments, and their results; knowing meant I had to have an interest in them and needed to ask after their families and their welfare. This was all too overwhelming, so I felt it was best to retire into a corner and maintain relationships only with doctors, nurses, and other St. Jude employees. This method, I believed, would best protect me from further emotional pain.

In spite of my best efforts, some patients and their families crept beyond the barriers I created. One such family was Russian, Alexander and his mother, Olga. They sat near us when I overheard their conversation in Russian, which immediately sparked my interest. I was brought up speaking German, but in my teenage years, I learned Russian in school and at home. When I was sixteen, my Ukrainian grandmother came to the United States at age sixty-eight to live with us. I wanted to speak with her, so I learned Russian on the fly.

I understood enough of what Olga was saying to Alexander to know he wanted gum, but she had none to give him. I broke my rules and introduced myself in Russian, asking if I could give Alexander a piece of my gum. She allowed him to take a piece from my pack, which made him very happy.

Of course, Olga was intrigued. How could there be someone at St. Jude on the Mississippi River speaking Russian? Her eyes lit up as we spoke. She later told me that our conversations made her feel less alone in a country that she did not understand.

Olga spoke English fairly well, so our conversations became an amalgamation of English-Russian. We both had holes in our understanding of our secondary language and were able to fill them in with our main language. Somehow, we managed to understand each other very well.

Alexander suffered from acute myeloid leukemia (AML), a

blood cancer that was difficult to treat. Olga and her husband had heard of St. Jude in Russia, as both of them were research doctors at the Leningrad hospital and had exchanged work with St. Jude in the past.

During Alexander's treatment, Olga kept meticulous spreadsheets of everything that was happening to him, from temperature to blood readings. As it turned out, Barry and Alexander were often hospitalized at the same time, giving Olga and me time to talk and carry on together. Sometimes I was able to act as translator when understanding between Olga and others became difficult. I believe that God puts us in situations where we can help. This was one of those situations.

Sometimes Olga and I escaped from the hospital to feel "normal." Two days before New Year's Eve proved to be one of our more memorable escapes.

We both were scheduled to leave for our respective homes for New Year's. At that time, Olga and Alexander were living in an apartment with some nuns on Poplar Avenue. Brian and the boys stayed at home on this night because Barry and I would be coming home in the morning.

During dinner, Olga and I reminisced about past New Year's Eves. She told me about a beautiful, red silk, mid-calf-length dress she wore the evening that she and her tux-outfitted husband went to dinner and then to the opera in a horse-drawn carriage. That sounded so romantic and exotic to me. She also wore a fur stole, as it was quite cold.

The most exotic New Year's I had ever spent was in New York City, where we met college friends, ate dinner in a lovely place, and went to an off-Broadway show. I wore a Christmas-green, sleeveless gown with a slit and silver platforms. After the show, we went to a small restaurant with a band where an older couple was cutting the rug—dancing with such enjoyment.

After exchanging memories of some more past experiences,

I said we should have our own lovely New Year's party. Olga laughed, hesitated, but then agreed if we could get the nurses in the ICU to check on the boys more often. The latter was a rather ludicrous thought as St. Jude's ICU nurses are the most committed, compassionate people on this planet! Nevertheless, we trotted upstairs with a childlike excitement I hadn't experienced in some time. Two of our favorite nurses were on duty that night and told us to go. They would not allow things to fall apart. (How ironic is that?)

We first went to Goldsmith's at Oak Court Mall on Poplar. There, we immediately headed for the evening gown department. Without hesitation, we snatched the most beautiful gowns off the rack and bustled toward the dressing rooms. I never thought about the look of sneakers and evening gowns, but we didn't care! We giggled and laughed as we modeled one gown after another for each other. There were gowns I couldn't zip up, so I held them together as I twirled in front of the mirror and Olga; others allowed far too much of my bosom to spill over, which caused us to belly-laugh so hard we cried; most were far too long.

Then, we both disappeared one more time into our dressing rooms, only to reappear together. Olga wore a deep-red, velvet and satin gown with three-quarter sleeves and with sequins on the bodice; I wore a sleek, forest-green number with an open back and long sleeves. I held my breath as we looked at each other in the trifold mirror. The momentary silence took us both back to far happier times. I wanted to cry and mumbled something about how this didn't exactly fit the evening as I ran back to the dressing room with tears stinging my eyes.

When I finally emerged, Olga was standing with an armful of glittering evening gowns, ready to return them to the rack. I took my lot, and as we hung up each gown, I thought of Cinderella and the midnight hour.

We left Goldsmith's in silence, each in our own reverie. My

thoughts turned to grief, wondering how many more New Year's Eve celebrations our children would have and if Olga and I would ever experience another wonderful, memorable New Year's.

In the car, I asked Olga if she wanted to take a carriage ride to The Peabody hotel or get a drink. She declined and said she wanted to return to Alexander. Secretly, I was glad she didn't want to continue the evening because I, too, felt that something in our lives had passed, never to be replicated again.

Yet, this joyous, reflective evening when we played dress-up at Goldsmith's will also never be replicated, and it was one of my favorite memories of our time at St. Jude. For a moment, we left behind the horror of our children's risk of death and gratefully remembered a softer, kinder life experience.

Olga, Alexander, Barry, and I were in the hospital together again a few weeks after New Year's. The boys each had scans, various chemo treatments, appointments, and so on. After the appointments, we went to the Crowne Plaza Hotel for the evening. We decided to go to dinner on Beale Street and then drive around a bit.

Because I am sometimes directionally challenged, I took some wrong turns, which amused Alexander to no end. He was so pleased that I didn't know where I was going and laughed so heartily that I continued to stay lost for an hour. We were howling like maniacs because his laughter was so infectious. When I finally stopped at the restaurant, we were totally sapped of any energy we might have had to eat. We got McDonald's instead and went back to crash into bed!

The next day, Olga told me that she was so grateful for Alexander's laughter. She had not heard him laugh so much since he became ill. My sides were hurting as well. When life is so difficult that you can't laugh, find those moments that make you laugh out loud. The physical and mental relief lifts the darkness and allows you to come to terms with the disorder in life.

I have difficulty coming to terms with disorder. I want things to turn out as I planned them. I want to be able to fix things easily. My center was not holding up. The collapse was imminent. What was I to do?

Both Alexander and Barry were installed in the ICU again. Both had low blood counts, possible infections, mouth sores, and bleeding noses. I learned that frozen bacon fat stuffed into a bleeding nostril heals the wound quickly. With all the modern techniques and medications available, it is plain bacon fat that does the trick. Amazing!

The second evening of another all-nighter, I met Olga on the walkway overlooking the Mississippi River and the lit bridge between Arkansas and Tennessee. We stopped to talk a bit. Alexander's blood count was extremely low, and he was running a high fever. The dark circles under Olga's eyes gave away her lack of sleep, and the flat look gave away her worry. I would hate for someone to tell me what I looked like!

As we talked about the boys and the difficulties facing them, I felt that Olga had more than cancer treatments on her mind. After a long silence while we watched traffic and the lit bridge, she asked me whether I prayed. I replied, "Yes. All day. All night. My prayer never stops."

Olga said that she had never prayed. In Russia, churches and anything else to do with God and prayer were ill-advised and practically outlawed. Although there was an underground network of Christians, Olga and her family never participated or practiced any Christian beliefs.

Olga wondered if I could teach her to pray. This was an unusual request because it had never occurred to me that someone would not know how to pray. I told her that I talked to God and asked that He heal Barry, give me strength, heal the other children at St. Jude, and help the doctors and nurses, and then it occurred to me that I was being selfish—again.

Perhaps, Olga should learn the Lord's Prayer, for isn't that what we should pray? In that moment, I asked if she would like to pray the Lord's Prayer with me. I said a line and then she said a line:

> Our Father, who art in heaven,
> Hallowed be Thy name.
> Thy Kingdom come.
> Thy will be done on earth,
> As it is in heaven.
> Give us this day our daily bread,
> And forgive us our trespasses,
> As we forgive those who trespass against us.
> And lead us not into temptation,
> But deliver us from evil.
> For Thine is the kingdom,
> And the power, and the glory,
> For ever and ever.
> Amen

I asked Olga if she would like to continue praying. She said no and went into her room. In those days, the parent and patient rooms were divided by a glass partition. The parent room was furnished with a sofa and chair, while the patient room had a hospital bed and wooden rocker. In order to enter the patient room, you had to walk around to the entrance of the ICU, wash your hands, and, depending on the patient's circumstance, wear a gown, gloves, and mask or simply wash your hands before you entered. Olga went to the parent room and quietly closed the door behind her.

I remained on the glass walkway and continued to watch the night traffic. As I looked out, I wondered what I believed about prayer. Certainly, I believe in the power of prayer, but somehow, I could not have my usual God conversation; instead, I remained silent. I was trying to listen, to sift through the clutter in my mind and hear God. "Be still, and know that I am God," Psalm 46 says.

As I looked out into the light-studded blackness of the river, the repetition of the words "Be still" became a prayer. Discerning God's voice is often tricky, but in the stillness, in the darkness of the night, I saw with clarity God's truth. He is with us, with me. No amen-caboose is needed.

I returned to Barry and crawled onto the bed with him, which was verboten, but the nurses allowed it because he slept much better when he had a fistful of my hair clutched in his hand. I slept fitfully like a dog at the end of the bed, glad that I could comfort him in this way. My open-ended prayer thanked God for another day of life.

Chapter 5

The Fall of the Berlin Wall

On November 9, 1989, Barry was still in the ICU after having low blood counts and a burgeoning infection. Sleep deprivation was contributing to my depression again. Each day, I wondered if this was the last day of his life. I was afraid to fall asleep in case I missed the catastrophic event of losing him.

Because rest eluded me, I turned the television on low as not to disturb Barry's fitful slumber. What I saw sent me into a spiral of emotion that swirled within me like a tornado!

I saw East and West Berliners flocking to the wall, drinking beer and champagne, and chanting, "*Tor auf!*" ("Open the gate!"). At midnight, thousands flooded through Checkpoint Charlie and the other gates. More than two million people from East Berlin visited West Berlin that weekend to participate in a celebration that was, one journalist wrote, "The greatest street party in the history of the world." People used hammers and picks to knock away chunks of the wall. Media began calling them *Mauerspechte*, or "wall woodpeckers," from the sound their tools made chipping at concrete as cranes and bulldozers pulled down section after section.

I could not believe my eyes! Was this really happening? I was glued to the TV for the next few days, soaking in all the information the media provided. I kept trying to tell Barry what the reporters were saying about one of the most important events of the century. He would have none of it because he wanted to watch baseball. After a day or so, I finally gave in and let him watch one game before I hogged the TV again.

In that interlude, I thought back to 1975, when I took a group of high school students from Batavia, New York, to Berlin and other German destinations, including Dachau, a concentration camp outside of Munich. I felt it was imperative that what I taught them was true and meaningful in a way that would touch them to the core.

The day we were to enter Berlin was filled with anxiety as I had never gotten the chance to see the wall in person. Each of us had to buy a day visa in order to step into East Berlin. We rode our comfortable bus from West Germany through East Germany to Berlin. When we reached the border, the East German guards made us give up our passports and visas. This made me nervous, for those papers were our lifeline to the United States. Without them, we could be held indefinitely by the Communist regime.

My German cohort teacher calmed me, saying it was simply protocol for them to check each person's identity. He had been to East Berlin often, so I assumed he was telling the truth. I was nervous because I had twenty-five students with me for whom I was responsible. My joke that bringing back 80 percent would make for a successful trip in my estimation suddenly did not seem so funny.

After some time, the guards returned with all our passports and visas and brought two large Rottweilers on board with them. One guard gave me all the paperwork and had me sign an affidavit that I was an American schoolteacher bringing students for a day trip to East Berlin. Meanwhile, the Rottweilers finished sniffing us and left.

The last event of import occurred when the guards rolled a large mirror contraption under the bus to check for any unwanted interlopers. The border-crossing process unnerved me, and I could see in the eyes of my students—with the exception of David, our senior class clown—an uncertainty that had not been evident before. When we were underway again, my blood pressure returned to normal. I thought, *That wasn't so bad!*

Some students talked quietly among themselves; others were writing the events in their journals. To this day, I wonder if some of those students are alive and still have their journals from that most intriguing week we spent together in East and West Germany.

Crossing from East Germany into West Berlin was far less stressful. Once we were installed in our hotel, we took a short tour of the Kurfürstendamm, the main street of Berlin. We saw a city that was vibrant and open twenty-four hours a day. There were lots of neon lights and signs, and people rushed to and fro, apparently busy getting to their destinations. We stopped at the best *Konditorei* (coffeehouse) in the world, the Café Kranzler. The students and I ordered delectables of all kinds. I remember having a piece of *Sahnetorte* (creme cake) and a delicious cup of coffee.

Everything seemed so civilized; yet, in the back of my mind, I wondered how Berliners were able to thrive, knowing what had happened here and what was over the wall that caged them inside. I spoke to one Berliner who essentially told me he stayed in West Berlin because "somebody has to." Isn't that true for so many situations? It takes a person of courage and total belief to do the hard things in life.

The next day, we took the only subway that led to the Communist side of Berlin. As the colorful billboard ads on the subway walls flashed by in a blur, I thought that East Berlin would not be much different from West Berlin. Boy, was I wrong!

After some time, the colorful billboards disappeared and were replaced by gray-black stone whizzing by. When we got off the subway, we were led down a tunnel to a room with a series of blackened windows that only had a small opening at the bottom, much like the ticket windows of a movie theater. As each person came to a blackened window, he inserted his passport and visa into the opening. In turn, each received a ticket that granted him entrance into East Berlin.

The guards in the room divided our group into two, along with a number of other people who were with us on the subway. I was not enamored by the idea of splitting our group, but my German cohort told me not to worry.

Before long, we were ushered into another room that had several long tables with guards behind each one. We were told to empty our pockets, purses, bags, or any other items we were carrying and to take off our coats, sweaters, hats, and shoes. This seemed extreme to me, but when in Rome . . .

I brought up the rear of my group, while my German cohort led the way. When my turn came to empty the contents of my bag, the guard asked how much money I was bringing to East Berlin. I gave him an approximate amount in German. He began counting my money and then decided that another guard should take me and my belongings elsewhere. Without a second thought, I explained in German that I was with the twenty-five students who had just gone through the inspection and asked if I could please follow them. He looked at me steadily and said that I must go with the other guard.

My cohort had told me not to argue with anyone, so I followed a guard who led me to a room that looked much like a doctor's room in a clinic. There was a table; a wooden chair; blank, dingy walls; and no window. The guard took my belongings and left me. What next?

I sat in the room for a short time, waiting for the guard to release me. Soon, I got annoyed and decided to peek out the door, as my son often did when he got tired of waiting for the doctor to see him. I turned the knob, but the door did not budge. The guard had locked me in!

Suddenly, the pit of my stomach lurched. I thought, *You have got to be kidding me!* In full panic, I started banging on the door and yelling, "Somebody open this door at once!"

No one came. After I grew tired and realized that no one was coming, I sat in the chair, truly fearing I was about to be arrested. I imagined myself never seeing my husband, son, and other family and friends again and rotting in some Communist dungeon for the rest of my days. Of course, I prayed that I would be saved from this misery. When my panic was fully in bloom, the door opened. A different guard entered with my coat and purse. In German, he said, "You are not very intelligent for a schoolteacher, are you? You don't seem to be able to count your money."

I responded in German, "I have given an approximate amount."

He sneered and told me to gather my things and leave. I gladly complied. As I stepped out into the sunlight of the day, I saw my group of students and cohort awaiting me. I was so glad to see them! I could have kissed each one, but then I saw their looks of concern and, yes, panic in their eyes.

We were allowed to walk around the impressive Alexanderplatz, which looked new and untouched by bombs or fire. It was the showpiece of East Berlin, and the Communists wanted visitors to see how very modern East Berlin was. This was all a ruse on their part to make Westerners believe an untruth, because beyond the pristine Alexanderplatz was dilapidated East Berlin.

As we walked along the streets, we saw guards carrying machine guns almost on every corner. We also saw storefronts showing the latest fashions and a few restaurants offering foods at exorbitant prices.

While we walked, I told my cohort that I could not be held up again on the way out. My students were frightened that their leader would not be able to return with them, and, frankly, I was frightened as well. He suggested that we go to the American consulate after lunch and tell the ambassador about the situation. Perhaps he could help in some way to ensure a smooth departure. I thought this was a good idea.

We lunched in an outdoor cafe at Alexanderplatz, where I saw two American soldiers in full uniform drinking beer at a nearby table. I was never so glad to see Americans in my life! The soldiers were on duty. It was their job to sit in an Alexanderplatz cafe for up to six hours daily to do nothing but be visible. The small but powerful presence of these two young Americans in full US army regalia made all the difference, at least to me.

I told them of my situation. The soldiers said that part of the Cold War was to make Americans feel uncomfortable when they visited East Berlin. They believed I was a perfect specimen because the delay could make my students worry and relay this information to people back in the States. I asked them to call my husband if I should be held up again. We exchanged phone numbers and addresses before I paid a visit to the ambassador. When everyone finished lunch, my cohort took my students on a tour while the two American soldiers escorted me to the embassy.

I was again living something movie-like, something unreal. The soldiers dropped me off and went to find the group and bring them to me while I spoke with the secretary of the embassy of the United States of America, Lewis Arthur Kert. At the top of the stairs, two US Marines with guns guarded the front door of the embassy. Another guided me to the secretary's office, which was outfitted in dark paneling and leather. A large, shiny desktop held only a black and red phone—nothing else. The whole incident reminded me of James Bond.

I didn't sit long before a handsome man with graying hair and a gray suit shook my hand in greeting. We wasted no time getting to the crux of the matter. After he listened to my tale, he picked up the receiver of the red phone, turned his chair so that his back was to me, and spoke quietly into the receiver in German. I could discern some of the conversation but not enough to know exactly what he said.

When the ambassador finished his conversation, he opened his desk drawer and wrote a number on a small business card. He slid the card across the slick desk to me and said, "Give this number to one of your students. If you are held up again at the exit, have the student call this number immediately after he has exited. This time, instead of bringing up the rear of the group, stand somewhere in the middle. Let the student who has the number go before you."

He assured me that I would have no difficulty. I asked why the Communists were so interested in me, and he reiterated what the soldiers said about the Cold War. I told him that I thought my mother had worked for the CIA, but I wasn't sure. I wondered if her position had anything to do with my situation, but he did not think so. Much later, I learned that my mother had read sensitive Russian materials for the CIA and that she was to report to her boss about anything suspicious she found in her reading.

I thanked him for assisting me, and he told me that it was his job to help Americans and be present in East Berlin. He said he only had a few more weeks of duty there before another ambassador would take over. Apparently, they worked in two-year stints, as being in East Berlin at the time was highly stressful. We shook hands, and when I exited the building, my group was awaiting me.

Everyone was ready to leave because they did not like seeing soldiers with guns or feeling like they were being watched at every turn. My cohort said we were to leave at five; leaving sooner would probably not be a good idea. We stopped at another small cafe for a drink before going to the subway station.

While everyone ordered, I took David to the side and told him

I needed him to help me if, for some reason, I was delayed again at the exit point. He was very willing to take part in this intrigue. I made him go to the restroom with me, take off his sneaker and sock, insert the card with the number, and look like being in the restroom with his teacher was the most natural thing to do! He left the restroom first, and I exited a few minutes later.

On our way to the subway, I stayed away from David, but I saw how he managed to walk like Quasimodo dragging his foot every time he saw me glance toward him. I could have slapped him silly!

We lined up to get our passports back from one of the blacked-out movie-theater windows. We each inserted our tickets, and in turn, our passports were returned. I saw that David had made it through the turnstiles past the guards and felt much relief. The retrieval of the passports went smoothly, but my turn was coming up. My jittery nerves held on tightly to the ticket. I inserted it. Did I imagine that my passport slid through the opening very slowly? I grabbed my passport and held myself back from galloping through the turnstiles. Once I was through, I cried and hugged David and the other students with all my might. We had learned valuable lessons about the Cold War that day.

Back in Barry's room, I watched on the TV as thousands of people streamed into the West. The exhilaration and hope that the people exuded at that moment made me believe anything was possible. I was reminded of walking along the wall in West Berlin with David Brown in 1975. He asked, "Mrs. Fowler, do you think this wall will ever come down?"

I answered, "It probably will not happen in our lifetime, but it will someday."

That someday was being played out before my eyes in St. Jude's ICU Room No.13.

On June 12, 1987, in a speech delivered from the Brandenburg Gate in West Germany, US President Ronald Reagan made one of his most famous statements when he called on Soviet Union leader

Mikhail Gorbachev to tear down the Berlin Wall. Today, it was happening. I wanted to call David and tell him how wrong I was, but I believe he thought about us as well and was celebrating with Germany's people.

As a side note, Gorbachev addressed more than two thousand West Tennessee residents in Jackson's Carl Perkins Civic Center during Union University's Fourth Annual Scholarship Banquet held on Tuesday evening, October 10, 2000. His speech centered on glasnost, political openness, perestroika, and governmental restructuring.

My friend Joan Livingston, a professor at Union, told me Gorbachev had accepted the invitation to speak, and Matt Williams, a local businessman, asked if I wanted to sit at the table with Gorbachev and other local dignitaries because I spoke some Russian. Of course, I wanted to sit with him and his daughter! Unfortunately, I was unable to sit with them because of some regulations, but Matt did arrange for me to be one of the people who were allowed to speak with Gorbachev after the program.

I had Gorbachev's wife Raisa's book in tow and wanted him to sign it. When it was my turn to speak with him, I blurted out my little Russian speech. Gorbachev and his entourage were surprised that someone from little Jackson, Tennessee, spoke Russian. When I requested his signature on the book, he declined because he said he does not sign anything.

My disappointed look must have stirred his daughter because she punched him gently on his shoulder and said, "Dad, sign the book. Do it for Mama!" Well, the power of daughters is far greater than a request from an unknown, Southern, Russian speaker. Gorbachev's picture taken with me on that night and his signature are among my treasured possessions.

As I reflect on all that I witnessed and experienced between 1989 and 2000, I cannot help but see God's hand in our world and in our lives.

Intervention 1

The Herons

D espair hit hard after eight months of cancer treatments, surgeries, sleepless nights, and growing fear that Barry was indeed going to die because of this alien force called neuroblastoma. The doctors of St. Jude felt it was important for patients, parents, and those working with both to take time off at Christmas, if possible.

We were sent home with the usual laundry list of do's and don'ts and a backpack for Barry to wear that injected much-needed antibiotics through his port. The family would have five days together before we were to return to another round of cisplatin chemotherapy and nights and days filled with worry.

Brian, Grandma, and I tried to make Christmas memorable for Ben and Brad. We put up the Christmas tree, bought and wrapped gifts, and prepared cookies, pies, and fresh cranberry salad, along with all the other usual seasonal pleasures that were our traditions. I was sleepwalking through the process, as I had no joy in my heart nor any desire to create these memories. Brian and Grandma insisted that I at least pretend for everyone and make this Christmas, perhaps our last together, a very special time.

How could I pretend to enjoy myself when everything in my world was wrong? The future looked bleak; the present was wrought with fear; the past was filled with frustration. If Brian and Grandma wanted to pretend, that was fine with me, but they should not expect me to gloss over the reality we were facing. No, I was not one for pretense.

In retrospect, I wish I had some of Brian's and Grandma's ability to sweep the negative, the uncomfortable, and the unpleasant under the carpet. Grandma cackled often, even when there was no reason to laugh. I believe her cackles, along with a little Valium, were a mechanism that she used throughout her entire life to keep everything smoothly sailing. It annoyed me to no end!

Again, my impudence should have been slapped out of me. Who was I to judge how someone navigated her way through the murky waters of life? My way wasn't that great!

When Christmas Eve approached and we put the boys down for the night, I could not read the goodnight story to Brad or talk about the exciting events of the next morning.

Circling in my mind was the fear of Barry's seemingly inevitable death in the coming year. I knew it would come that year because all the literature indicated that neuroblastoma took most children who were diagnosed after the age of one within a year or two of diagnosis. Barry's disease was Stage D when it was discovered, which meant it had already spread into his small bones. What chance did he have? I was certain the outcome of his treatment would be death, and that was the focus of my thoughts.

On the quiet, dark Christmas Eve of 1989, I prayed for a miracle: "God, if You are real, if You exist, if You are who You say You are, then please, please save Barry. I have so little to offer in return, but I will do anything so that he has a chance at life."

The adage that hindsight is 20/20 truly applies to me. The inability to think ahead or comprehend the importance of the present is a huge flaw in my character. Probably, many of us suffer from this flaw with no prospect of correcting it. How much more confusing life would be if we were able to see the future! The decisions we would make to avoid or avert certain events could conjure up a whole series of other events that might be worse than the originally intended ones. Ugh! I couldn't stand it!

I struggled through the night, having given up on sleeping pills some time ago. By six, the boys were ready for the chaos of Christmas morning. Because I had to change Barry's port dressing first and get him ready, the boys had to wait for the grand opening.

Our tradition was that Brian and I always drank coffee, our morning tonic, while we watched the fun of tearing, screeching, and all-around mayhem that ensued. As I prepared the coffee, I looked outside and teared up as I saw a blue heron staunchly keeping watch over the edge of the pond. Before I knew it, I was sobbing uncontrollably over the sink, wanting nothing more than for everything to go away. The pain hurt so deeply that I ran from the boys and Brian to the bathroom.

One of the boys asked, "Why are you crying, Mom?"

Between sobs, I blurted out, "It's not snowing!"

I sat on the toilet, trying to gather my wits, but the tears continued to stream nonetheless. My weeping stopped when I heard the boys screaming in a way that mothers know requires their attention. Something had happened, and I knew that Barry was involved. Quickly, I pulled myself together to tend to the newest emergency.

Brad was waiting outside the bathroom door, wanting me to take his hand. I looked for the catastrophe without seeing. Nothing seemed to be amiss until everyone shouted, "Look!"

We forgot all about the gifts and the weeping because we saw the biggest snowflakes floating over the pond, heron, and yard. No snow was predicted for our cotton field, but there it was. What a Christmas gift! We were so joyous about this beautiful, unexpected winter scene that I immediately got my camera to take pictures of this most wondrous sight. To this day, my favorite picture of that day is Brad with arms spread wide, a big smile, and a silver bow stuck on his red toboggan catching snowflakes in his mouth.

Suddenly, things couldn't be more right!

As with most things, I am never satisfied. After the excitement of the morning snowfall and the gift-opening havoc dissipated, the boys played with their new toys, and I went to work in the kitchen on our traditional turkey dinner. Brian was removing the giblets and neck from the turkey when I felt the dark cloud of depression from earlier in the morning overwhelming me again. I looked over Brian's shoulder out of the window at the stately heron, still holding down the edge of the pond. He looked ephemeral through the scrim of thick snowflakes, and he seemed lonely. In an instant, tears emerged again.

Brian's look of concern was not enough to keep me from crying. Apparently, the boys heard my sniffles and stood before me in stairstep fashion, wondering what they should do or say.

"The heron looks lonely to me," I said.

"What? You want to invite him in for turkey dinner?" Brian asked. The boys snickered.

"No, I just wish he had a mate or friend, someone to be with him today," I answered.

Seeing that my crying bordered on the absurd, the boys went back to their toys, and Brian continued wrestling with the turkey. I told him I would lie down a bit in hopes that I would feel better later. Being tired but unable to sleep is one of the worst feelings in the world. Yet, that morning, I had wiped myself out with so little sleep and so much maudlin emotion that I actually dozed off.

My momentary hiatus was short-lived. Once again, the alarm

sounded from the kitchen. The boys screamed, "Go get Mom! Hurry, hurry!"

Again, my mom antennae zeroed in on the emergency. I jumped out of bed, ran to the kitchen, and found all three boys' faces plastered to the glass door facing the pond. I stood over them watching a sight I had never seen before and have not seen since that Christmas of 1989. Walking over the berm next to the pond, our blue heron appeared. With long strides, he marched through the daylily bed and stood in the center of the yard with snow falling steadily around him. He stood perfectly still, gazing directly at us, and we at him. We were mesmerized by his presence and his absolute perfection.

Then, we all inhaled simultaneously because a white head with long feathers bounded over the berm. The ghostly white heron stood next to our blue heron in the swirling snow; the melancholy woman and steadfast birds exchanged silent words. "Thank you."

The birds scampered about in the yard, playing a game of chase, and eventually flew away together. The talk for the rest of the day centered on the snow, the herons, and on what the event could mean. For me, the meaning was clear. God had spoken to me in his own inimitable way. I was not alone in this crisis and never would be.

The relief I felt was outstanding. I was so grateful for my little family but mostly for a God who saw fit to help a struggling ant on this dirt ball on which we live. Christmas 1989 would remain the most memorable Christmas we ever experienced.

Chapter 6

A Night of Reality

I had been in inpatient with Barry for almost two weeks. We were all getting testy because we were confined to his room with only a hard-backed oak rocker and his bed.

I slept at the end of Barry's bed like a dog for the duration of his isolation. In those days, parents were supposed to sleep on the other side of a glass partition between the patient room and the parent room. The faux leather, flat sofa in the parent room was no more comfortable than sleeping at the end of his bed. The nurses looked the other way when I settled in for the night with Barry. He clutched my hair in his little hands and fell soundly asleep. When I was not in bed with him at night, he refused to sleep and, on several occasions, ripped his tubing out of his chest and arms.

To be honest, I felt much better sleeping with Barry because I couldn't stand watching him through the glass as though he was some kind of specimen or zoo animal. He needed me as much as I needed him.

Barry's behavior while in inpatient caused the hospital to change several rules. The main change was that St. Jude began allowing parents to stay in the room with the patient rather than on the other side of the glass partition.

After Barry's first surgery to remove cancer from his abdomen, he was in bad shape. He had multiple bags with drugs, blood, plasma, and saline being infused into his body. Since everything couldn't go through his port, he had an IV in his arm. When he did not see me in his room but behind the glass partition, he became super upset, pulled out every tube, and knocked over the whole contraption, pole, and bags. Blood spurted out of his port incision in his chest; he screamed bloody murder until I returned to him. He caused so much havoc that I was instructed to stay with him henceforth.

Because of the damage Barry caused with his temper tantrum, he had to have surgery again to insert a Hickman line. Apparently, the doctors and nurses decided that keeping mother and child separated was more trouble than it was worth. When things settled down, I got into bed with Barry nightly, and nothing else was said about it.

Usually, Brian relieved me for a few hours each night so I could shower and get out of the hospital, even though he was exhausted from driving so often between Jackson and Memphis. On this particular weekend, I said, "Why don't you stay home to catch up on some much-needed sleep in your own bed? Maybe you can find time to do something fun with the boys. They need you, too."

For some reason, Barry's blood was acting up that night. The following day, his room was a revolving door. Nurses, doctors, techs, and others came to do whatever they needed to do to insert a needle into his rolling veins. He was pricked often and cried most of the night and day. Neither of us slept.

When the constant searching for veins slowed, Barry calmed down. The blood emergency seemed to have passed, but I was far from being settled. There comes a point after you haven't slept that you can't fall asleep, and if you do, sleep is fitful and totally unsatisfying. By late afternoon on Saturday, Barry finally gave in to sleep, and I decided to go to the cafeteria for coffee and a hamburger.

As I stepped out of the elevator, I met Dr. Abraham, a woman with six children and a stay-at-home husband. I liked her because she never couched what was happening to Barry in doctor speak or in gibberish I couldn't understand. Dr. Abraham took one look at me and told me to wait a second while she made some phone calls. I heard her talking to her husband and then the ICU nurse.

After her calls, she turned to me and smiled. "Let's get out of here. You look like hell!"

"Oh, really!" I said. "Thanks, but no thanks. I've got to be here in case Barry wakes up."

"Barry is being well taken care of, and we won't be long. I'm taking care of you for a bit," she said.

Overwhelmed, I began to cry upon hearing that. Dr. Abraham ushered me to her car in the doctors' parking area of the garage, put me in the front seat, and let me cry, while offering me clean Kleenex and a garbage bag for my used ones. She was an old hand at dealing with crisis.

What triggered my outburst was the fact that someone said, "Let me take care of you." How often I felt the burden of handling everything going on with Barry at St. Jude, worrying about Brian working and driving, worrying about the boys and Grandma, worrying about our finances, worrying about so much. The weight pressed on my shoulders. Dr. Abraham had been on duty for the past four days and noticed my emotional decline. Thank God!

I didn't ask where we were going. It didn't matter. I wanted to cry and be with someone who understood and didn't care.

We arrived at The Peabody within a few minutes. Dr. Abraham informed me that we were going to have a glass of wine and some civilized conversation that did not entail blood counts, scans, or anything hospital-related. Dressed in my jeans and St. Jude T-shirt with Dr. Abraham in her scrubs and white coat, we settled in a corner of the magnificent Peabody lobby, where the fountain, complete with ducks and enormous, fresh flower arrangements, presented an elegant atmosphere.

The lobby was a far cry from the sterile, white surroundings of Barry's inpatient room. The bar at one end of the lobby displayed glimmering glassware with bottles of every size and color; at the other end of the lobby, a pianist played a jazzy number on the baby grand. I huddled in a soft leather chair, aware that I was not appropriately dressed for such an elegant place, but that did not deter Dr. Abraham from ordering two glasses of chardonnay from the waiter.

While we awaited our wine, Dr. Abraham told me about her family and her arrangement with her husband, who was willing to be the stay-at-home parent to rear their children. She talked mainly about the antics her children produced daily, but I had difficulty taking in what she was saying.

The wine arrived, and we toasted to the moment, this evening at the luxurious Peabody. Dr. Abraham suggested I drink the wine slowly because she was only paying for one glass each and because she intended to return me to St. Jude in one piece.

As we sipped from the light golden liquid, I surveyed the lobby over the rim of my glass. A middle-aged, well-dressed couple was engaged in an animated discussion in low tones. Perhaps, they were arguing over something important or something inconsequential. At one end of the bar, two young men dressed in trendy outfits toasted each other; at the other end of the bar, a white-haired businessman brooded over his scotch on the rocks. My eyes moved counterclockwise and found other people engrossed in each other:

two lovebirds sat close to one another murmuring softly; three well-heeled women discussed new fashion trends; a man with furrowed brow studied his pager. And, of course, here I sat wondering if others created stories about these two out-of-place women.

Dr. Abraham stopped talking while I took mental pictures of the people in the room. When I finished my surveillance, she asked me to tell her what I saw. I created stories about the various groups and individuals who shared the same breathing space that we did. For example, I surmised that the young couple was beginning a long evening of love and romance. The woman who laughed coyly at her lover's comments over the top of her fizzy drink was definitely preparing to take him up on an offer he was about to make as he lightly stroked her bare arm with his lovely, long fingers. I hoped their night would end in each other's arms where both could feel safety, warmth, and love.

My attention drifted to the brooding man with his scotch. I wondered what baggage his life made him carry: divorce, loneliness, addiction? Then, the well-heeled, middle-aged women talked excitedly about going to the Orpheum Theatre for a program. They waved their manicured hands in the air as they spoke to accentuate a point or maybe to show off their jewels. They planned to go to Beale Street after the show. Again, I wondered what that would bring into their lives.

Dr. Abraham maintained they were out to be "girls" again like they once were, and perhaps a younger man would hit on one of them and that would make her day. Our stories took twists and turns and became bizarre. Perhaps the wine, the stories, or a combination caused us to giggle. For the first time in what seemed like ages, I had put St. Jude, Barry, and the ICU to the side.

As we downed the last of our wine, Dr. Abraham suggested that I remember this scene at The Peabody. We are simultaneously living life in our own spots in the world. Each of us has his own problems, his own decisions to make, his own relationships to foster, and his own reactions to the changes that life brings. That evening at The Peabody was a life lesson to me: Even though maintaining perspective may be difficult when a life event is overwhelming, it is good to remember that you are not alone.

Dr. Abraham dropped me off at the front doors of St. Jude and went home to hover over her brood. I learned a second valuable lesson from her that Saturday evening. Although she had worked many long hours herself and had been on her way home to her family, she opted to help a fellow human in distress. Her action has compelled me to follow suit.

We know about kindness and concern, but we often do not know how to go about acting in a kind manner ourselves. Until you have experienced such action and have internalized this yourself, you will not be able to perform in kind. The unselfish person who puts aside his desires for another is someone we should emulate. In my life so far, Dr. Abraham was the example, the teacher to whom I will forever be grateful for such valuable lessons.

When I returned to the ICU, Wendy, our nurse, said Barry had not peeped once. I crawled into bed with him, felt his small fingers grab a hank of my hair, and then I was out.

Chapter 7

Speeches

A fter we had spent four months at St. Jude, a counselor asked if I would speak to one of the many groups who visit to learn about the hospital and who want to help fund the children's care through ALSAC, the fundraising arm of St. Jude. Apparently, my big mouth impressed this counselor enough to ask me to speak.

On the other hand, not everyone who undergoes the trauma of having a child with cancer feels comfortable standing before an auditorium full of people who are eager to learn about what happens to a family in the throes of treatment. The counselor believed I would become a good spokesperson because, as a teacher, speaking to groups would not be a hardship for me.

Of course, I told him that I would be glad to tell our story to date; however, I did not feel comfortable discussing the medical aspects of Barry's treatment. That would not be a problem because a doctor would inform the audience of the technicalities; my job was to tell our story. Thus began a long line of speeches that I would give over two years.

While I sat with Barry through bone scans and MRIs or at night while he slept, I worked on a draft for the speech that I gave repeatedly, making adjustments as time passed and other events occurred.

The following is part of the speech I gave initially. I would alter this same speech as life unfolded.

"The mythological Sisyphus was unfortunate enough to have witnessed Zeus, disguised as an eagle, carry the king's daughter away in his talons. He was so distraught that he immediately told the king. When Zeus discovered Sisyphus's betrayal, Zeus relegated him to forever rolling a rock up a hill, only for it to roll down on him as soon as he made it to the top, for all of eternity.

"Barry's and our story is much like Sisyphus's. In 1989, Barry, at age three and a half, was diagnosed with a rare childhood cancer called neuroblastoma. The cancer attacked the nervous system and had wrapped itself around all the major arteries in his abdomen, including the aorta. The doctors of St. Jude Children's Research Hospital only gave him a few months to live and told us to be prepared for his untimely death.

"Yet, after a little more than a year of high-dose chemotherapy, radiation, and surgeries, Barry was declared in remission. During that year, we often faced untold lows and highs when we rolled the proverbial rock. However, in each case, we were supported by doctors, nurses, staff, friends, and family."

The following are the note cards from my first speech after giving the above introduction:

1. Spring 1989, we began to roll our rock uphill.
   Beginning signs of illness.
   Interminable all-night crying.
   Weight loss.
   Stomach and leg pain.
   Multiple trips to doc.
2. Local physician says I must stop spoiling Barry unforgivable.
   8 weeks—ran from doc to doc.
   Specialist declares he has juvenile arthritis.
   After inconclusive Jackson hospital stay went to Le Bonheur.
   Wanted to send us home—I insisted we stay.
   Held Barry for days.
3. CT scan showed cancer.
   Don't trust multiple doctors coming to see you— bad news.
   Surrealistic day.
4. Drs. explained neuroblastoma.
   Childhood cancer, 1 in 10,000 develop it.
   Most often in abdomen, adrenal glands, or kidney.
   How much did I hear? Don't know. Too much info.
   They asked if I had ?'s.
5. 2 came to mind—
   a. Where were we to go now?
   b. How much would it cost to treat Barry?
   Perhaps you think me cold and insensitive to think of these two things, but I did not wish to waste time.
6. Dr. Meyer answered: St. Jude and ALSAC will take care of everything.

With answers in hand, I left the doctors sitting in their semicircle.

7. Returned to Barry's room—numb.

My drugged child lay in the bed peacefully for the first time in weeks.

Drs. followed me to room.

Called Brian. Come; it's cancer! Hung up.

8. Within minutes, two doctors from St. Jude were in Barry's room.

They assured me Barry would be well cared for and to go home for the weekend and return on May 8, 1989!

That day and subsequent days taught us about living and loving and seizing the day.

9. At home tried to explain situation to Grandma and the boys.

Shock, crying, worry.

10. Monday a.m. walked through the doors of St. Jude— our lives were indelibly altered.

Armband #11052; as of this speech # is over 13000 mark.

11. Mrs. Strom—insurance info. What ours doesn't cover will be covered by St. Jude.

Always truthful and to the point.

When Barry in hospital, all meals, gas, and accommodations paid for.

More relief.

12. From May '89–July '90, Barry had 20 hospital stays, 2 long surgeries, 30 days of radiation, countless MRIs, CT scans, bone scans, and lab procedures, not to mention visits with a variety of specialists.

The cost for such treatment is enormous.

You can imagine what a relief it was that these expenses were taken care of.

I quit my job.

13. After insurance paperwork, we were taken to Section C of hospital.

Dr. Garcia—"drug dealer from S. Am."

Love/hate relationship.

14. Medicine room aka Beauty Parlor—no one gets hair done.

Davey/throws up/eats Cheerios.

Mother chatting about *Days of Our Lives* on TV.

Panic—"Where am I?"

15. Cyclophosphamide; others followed.

Cisplatin.

Adriamyacin.

VM26.

Vocabulary increases quickly at St. Jude.

Meds will make Barry's beautiful curly hair fall out.

16. Remember Sisyphus's rock—well, it rolled way down.

Barry's blood count hit bottom overnight.

Needed IV with antibiotics; had no port.

17. Tedious, horrible night.

Nurse after nurse, doctors, phlebotomists, tried to put an IV in—all failed.

"Mommy, please make them stop!"

How do you tell your child this is for his own good? I wasn't convinced myself.

Finally, a Florence Nightingale succeeded; IV in ankle.

18. Brian arrived next a.m.; I'm exhausted, hadn't showered or slept in 2 days.

Lesson: important to take a break.

19. Brian drove daily from Jackson—2-hour round trip after going to work all day.

Barry rarely let me leave room.

Barry learned to bend hospital rules:

  a. Mom will sleep in my bed, not behind glass; jumped out of bed and pulled all IVs out after surgery.
  b. It was decided to let me stay with him.
20. Home support so important:
  a. "Cancer" shower.
  b. Housekeeper for a year; someone paid.
  c. Meals for a year; school friends.
  d. New tires for my car.
  e. Money in our account from anonymous sponsors.
21. Hospital support:
  a. Setup of hospital room complete with supplies and antibiotic backpacks; feedings, etc.
  b. Sibling Day.
  c. Drs. A and G; nurse practitioners E and R.
22. Radiation until end of June.
  Garcia throws us out.
  Addicted to St. Jude.
  Needed to drop the crutch of St. Jude.
23. How do you enter the world you once knew to be normal and be a part of it again? How do you gain access to the mainstream of life?
24. You people before me make the difference in the lives of so many of us at St. Jude.
25. "I shall be telling this with a sigh
  Somewhere ages and ages hence
  Two roads diverged in a yellow wood
  And I took the one less traveled by
  And that has made all the difference."

After quoting from Robert Frost's famous poem, I said in conclusion, "You make all the difference!"

Sometimes I passed out polished stones to remind the audience of our lot in life and to thank them for helping us roll the rock uphill.

Apparently, my short speeches made an impression on all who heard me. Sometimes I cried during the speech; other times, some in the audience cried. All seemed glad to hear a firsthand account of life in the cancer trenches, and I felt good knowing that I did have an impact on the people who came. They would go back to their communities and raise money so that St. Jude could continue to give superb care and service to its young patients and families. I was able to give back a little for all that the hospital had done for us and all the other patients.

My speech-making continued with basically the same story. Sometimes I added some humorous elements such as "Torch," one of our favorite nurses, who accidentally called the fire trucks from the fire station around the corner. Barry was on a gurney in the hallway so that she could give him a shot. Maggie tapped the fire alarm with the hypodermic needle to remove any bubbles in it, but she tapped a bit too hard. Chaos ensued, and everyone was expected to evacuate the building. Maggie's face turned red when she realized what she had done. Barry and I laughed. Luckily, Maggie knew whom to call to turn off the alarms. Whew! From that day on, Maggie became known as "Torch" throughout the hospital.

At the end of each speech, we would hold a question-and-answer session where the audience could ask the doctor or me anything they wished. Sometimes the speeches were held in the auditorium, and sometimes they were held in the Danny Thomas rotunda. Most often, I gave my speeches to everyday people who wanted to serve the hospital in some way. However, a few speeches were quite memorable.

The teachers' union of Tennessee was meeting at the Opryland Hotel in Nashville. This was a very important meeting for St. Jude because the teachers were to vote on whether to give their funds to St. Jude or to the Sickle Cell Association since sickle cell disease affected many children in the South. As a matter of fact, St.

Jude's efforts initially were to cure sickle cell anemia. During the program, I was nervous as the representatives of St. Jude, of which I was one, needed to do a super job in their presentations so the teachers' union would continue to subsidize St. Jude's efforts. At that time, St. Jude was studying sickle cell since the disease affected the blood as leukemia affected the blood. St. Jude's researchers were hoping to learn something from sickle cell disease that would help children with leukemia.

I was the second to last to speak. Hundreds of teachers were seated in two of Opryland's ballrooms, and it was definitely the largest crowd that I had ever addressed. As I looked out over the colorful landscape of faces, I could not distinguish one from another. My clammy hands and shallow breathing also made me uncomfortable. Then I thought of all the little faces at St. Jude whom I saw daily and knew I could soldier through my speech. No, I could nail this because it was so important to make the teachers understand the need for their contributions.

A nice round of applause thanked me for my words, but I believe the ALSAC director swung the teachers' votes to St. Jude's side when he explained St. Jude's efforts in the sickle cell area. I'm sure they felt they were helping both causes in this way. We were so relieved.

In the summer of 1990, I was asked to speak in Salt Lake City, Utah, at the Hilton Hotel at the Epsilon Sigma Alpha Sorority's annual meeting. This international group has supported St. Jude since 1972 and has given the hospital over $250 million in cash and pledges. The meeting was also a time when each chapter from various states assembled to conduct their business.

I was to speak at the final banquet, and after my speech, Terre Thomas, Danny Thomas's daughter, would be presented with a hefty check. By this time, I was gaining my stride and was excited to tell as many as I could about wonderful St. Jude.

After arriving in Utah, I discovered that my luggage went to

Montreal and would get back to me ASAP. I learned something on that trip: Always take a carry-on with you complete with underwear, toiletries, and Tylenol. I noticed a Victoria's Secret store in the hotel lobby and decided to purchase panties, three for ten dollars. I thought my suitcase would arrive the next day and all would be well.

The second day included a hayride into the mountains. Luckily, I was wearing traveling jeans that could go about anywhere, especially on a hayride. Of course, dinner would be another story. I thought most of these ladies wouldn't know me until Friday's banquet and I'd be all right with clean underwear. By dinnertime, I was feeling itchy, but I didn't think much about it.

By the second day, and especially after the hayride, my discomfort had increased. I attributed the itchiness on my thighs to the hay on the hayride and the heat of the day. I reasoned that a shower and a good night's sleep would make me feel better.

On Friday morning, a tour of the Salt Lake Tabernacle and other sightseeing options were available. The woman in charge of my lost luggage told me that my suitcases would arrive Friday afternoon. That was good, as the dress I planned on wearing at the fancy banquet was required. We spent all morning learning about the Mormons and their famous choir. I had hoped to hear the choir, but it was on a tour in Russia.

After lunch, we returned to the hotel, and lo and behold, my luggage was in my room. I could get dressed for the banquet, which would be a fancy affair with Terre Thomas scheduled to speak as well as me.

A chapter liaison picked me up, and I was seated at a table on the stage with other ESA dignitaries. Sitting among these women, whose mission was to help St. Jude Children's Research Hospital in its quest to eradicate childhood cancer, was humbling.

The woman on my right told me she had been a member of the organization for over ten years. She felt a need to help children after her son died in an unexpected accident. She found a home among many other women who had experienced the loss of a child or loved one. Her story and those of others in their community were heart-wrenching; yet, each of these women wanted to make the life of another child important. Again, I learned that I was not alone, which is often the fear one has when faced with a dangerous situation. They truly inspired me to make my talk worth their while.

Indeed, after the speeches, including mine, the president of the chapter gave Terre Thomas a check for $2.3 million. It took my breath away. As I looked over the sea of smiling faces, I wanted to weep. I told as many of them as I could how grateful I was for their efforts to help St. Jude's children. I could not have been loved more by complete strangers than I was that evening.

The St. Jude contingent was to leave after breakfast; however, I was having significant issues and needed medical treatment, so we did not leave until after lunch. Apparently, the panties I bought at Victoria's Secret had a dye in them to which I was allergic. My legs, all the way past my knees, were covered with reddish, leather-like skin that itched incredibly. Luckily, the group included several doctors, and I was able to get some relief. After two weeks or so, my skin was back to normal, but I was embarrassed by the whole episode.

My next big trip was to Dallas, Texas, not an overnight affair but a dinner. I never knew what to expect when I was sent to speak. This time, I was ushered to Morton's The Steakhouse across from the Book Depository. My St. Jude partner and I were taken to the steakhouse's basement, where a group of approximately ten to twenty people were seated and the dinner was about to commence. I was introduced, gave my speech, answered a few questions, and was whisked back to the airport to return to Memphis.

I never discovered who these people were to whom I spoke, but my St. Jude partner intimated that they were very generous

Texans. I concluded they must have been millionaires to have had such a special evening. Later, my partner told me that those people gave a generous sum to St. Jude. I didn't need to know more; my gratitude to them will stand by itself.

I continued to speak at St. Jude as groups from around the world came to visit the facility and hear about the latest research. Shortly after my Utah trip, something strange happened. We were close to finishing our first year of treatment. Barry had withstood two surgeries and many scary nights in the ICU, and now it seemed we were coming to an end.

Dr. Garcia, Dr. Patel, and Dr. Fein agreed that Barry should have radiation treatments daily for a month to kill any residual S cells that may be left in his abdomen. Of course, we agreed.

Then I was asked again to address a visiting group. As I talked, I found myself speaking in a monotone, or so it seemed to me. Brian said my speech sounded fine, but down deep inside, I felt like a stranger to what I was saying. Perhaps I sensed that our stay at St. Jude was coming to a close, or I was tired of repeating myself.

It was time to pass the baton of life at St. Jude in the face of death to another. I mentioned my feelings to the ALSAC person responsible for speakers, and he understood. I was not asked to speak again.

A closing thought to this part of our St. Jude adventure: Sometimes I feel guilty for expressing my feelings about not wanting to speak more. The people who work at St. Jude never once told me they were tired of their work or wished to pass the baton; rather, they were there every step of the way for us and for every other patient and family.

Chapter 8

A Visit From Danny Thomas

I n the spring of 1990, we were again in inpatient Room No.13, when a knock on the door alerted us to a visitor. We first saw a hand on the door with an unlit cigar held between the fingers. I almost fell out of my chair when the person stood in the doorway. Danny Thomas came in and asked if he could sit on Barry's bed. Barry had no idea who he was but smiled at him as though he was an old friend.

Danny did not speak to me but asked Barry if he could watch TV with him. We had started watching an episode of *The Three Stooges*. Danny told Barry that the Stooges were among his favorites, and he was glad to arrive in time to see them. Barry was munching on Cheerios and offered Danny some. He graciously declined.

I began to make small talk that soon annoyed him. He asked, "Would you like to get a cup of coffee? Barry and I are going to enjoy the Stooges." I got the hint and packed my purse to leave. When Barry saw my maneuver to go, I thought he would say something. He did not care, for he and Danny were busy with the Stooges.

I quietly left the room and took advantage of the time off even though I would have liked to ask questions about Danny's TV career. However, that career was merely a way to pay back St. Jude, patron saint of lost causes, for Danny promised to create the hospital if St. Jude helped him and his family and the children suffering from catastrophic diseases, particularly sickle cell anemia. Danny said, "Help me find my way in life and I will build you a shrine."

As I sat in the cafeteria drinking my coffee, I thought of the strength and fortitude Danny had to bring this wonderful hospital into existence. He was a man of his word. My thoughts wandered to immigrants like my own mother, who packed one suitcase between us and brought us to America after World War II. What tremendous resolve these immigrants had in order to leave their homes and start afresh in this melting-pot country so that they could give their families and themselves better lives. Their children were born Americans, like Danny. My rumination took longer than I expected before I headed back to Room No.13.

As I approached the sink to wash my hands and use the sanitizer outside the room, I heard two people chuckling and then howling. By this time, Barry had moved over to let Danny lounge next to him in the bed. I wish I had an iPhone back then to take a picture of the two having such a grand time.

When the show was over, Danny hugged Barry and gave me a little bow as he left the room. Barry asked, "Who was that man, Mommy?"

How could I explain to him that man made possible his treatment at St. Jude? That man was responsible for giving Barry and others like him a chance at life.

"You've just met a 'star,' " I said.

That seemed to suit him, and he continued his Stooges marathon.

At suppertime, Brian brought Ben and Brad to Memphis to see Barry and spend time with me. Often when we arrived at St. Jude, some organization brought toys to give the children. This time, miniature baseball bats signed by one player or another were distributed to the patients and their siblings. My guys were so excited. Everywhere you looked, a child was swinging a bat.

We decided to eat supper early so that I could do some shopping with the boys in Memphis. The cafeteria was already full, and in one corner sat Danny with several doctors and suits. He was always served his coffee in a cup and saucer rather than the paper cups the rest of us used. One empty table was close to him, so we took it.

Brian took Ben through the cafeteria line while Brad and I waited our turn. People were milling about and talking when I heard a loud "Whoa!"

I turned my head and saw Brad holding his baseball bat inches from Danny's head. He was about to take a good swing and knock Danny out! I could see the headlines: "Brad Fowler kills Danny Thomas, founder of St. Jude, with a mini baseball bat."

Of course, Brad had no idea that he was about to wreak havoc in the cafeteria. Danny was so kind to him. He called Brad over, talked, and told him how he enjoyed being with his brother. Luckily, I had my camera in my purse and got a snapshot of Danny and Brad. For the rest of the evening, Brad felt bad that he nearly did such a terrible thing. I told Brad he now had a story to tell that had a happy ending.

We never saw Danny again because he died in 1991. We attended his public funeral in Memphis, and he was laid to rest in a family burial crypt at the Danny Thomas/ALSAC Pavilion on the grounds of the hospital.

When we return to the hospital for our yearly visit, we stop to pay homage to Danny and to St. Jude Thaddeus.

Chapter 9

Make-A-Wish

I n February 1990, a woman named Mrs. Crawford from the Make-A-Wish Foundation asked to see us. We met with her in the hospital's waiting area. She explained that Barry qualified for a Make-A-Wish dream. I had heard of the foundation, but I never expected that Barry would be a recipient of such generosity.

"The doctors think Barry might be able to enjoy the gift soon," she added.

"Would you like to go to Disney World or get a computer or something else you've been wanting?" She smiled at Barry.

"If you go to Disney World," she said, looking at me, "the whole family will go all expenses paid."

I was astounded. Then it occurred to me that a four-year-old wanted his mom and dad and his favorite truck. He would be happy with that.

"Barry would like to go to Honolulu," I quipped.

She raised her gray eyebrows, looked at Barry, then at me, and said, "I don't think a four-year-old is interested in Mai Tais on the beach."

"You're right, of course," I agreed. "But at the same time, a four-year-old only wants to be with his parents and a few of his precious toys."

"I don't think a Hawaiian trip will be possible," she said quietly.

"Thank you, Mrs. Crawford, for such a generous offer, but we will decline," I said. "Perhaps an older child would be better suited for a trip to Disney World or a computer or other expensive item."

She studied us for a moment. "Well, I hope you'll think about it, and I'll come back at another time."

I detected that she was shocked that I did not accept her offering, but she merely packed up her paperwork and left. I did not give Mrs. Crawford or the Make-A-Wish Foundation another thought.

The weeks went by with the usual drill: chemo, low blood counts, inpatient, panic, and then a respite as Barry's blood counts increased. Then we were sent home one weekend for a change of scene with his usual backpack of IV antibiotics.

We were among the first to be entrusted with backpack antibiotics. Apparently, St. Jude thought we could handle intravenous feeding schedules and antibiotic treatment at home. We were guinea pigs to see if some patients and families could be successful in giving treatment at home. If so, hospital rooms could be used for other patients, and staff would be freed to treat others.

St. Jude set up my bedroom at home like a complete inpatient room with medical supplies, IVs, and other equipment. The intravenous feeding bags would be sent via FedEx daily. I was given specific instructions for everything and a direct line to a doctor if I needed help.

All went well initially, and we enjoyed being home with the boys and Dad. However, by Saturday night, Barry was spiking a high fever, which meant we had to return to St. Jude immediately. I called St. Jude to tell them we were on our way and that they should get Room No.13 ready! I rolled Barry in a blanket and put him on the passenger side of the car, and Brian stayed home with the other two boys.

By the time I got to Shelby County, I was clocking 90 mph. Barry was burning up, and there simply was no time to waste. Within minutes after I entered Shelby County, a police car was chasing me, with blue lights and a siren, telling me to pull over. I knew I had to stop, but I did not want to because every minute counted. When the policeman came to my side of the car to ask for my license, I quickly explained the situation.

He did not ask another question. He shouted, "Follow me!"

In that moment, I thanked God for the policeman. He escorted us at high speeds all the way to the garage of St. Jude and never gave me a ticket.

Barry was rushed to inpatient, and all the preparations for his care were made. I stood out in the hallway overlooking one of the river bridges to catch my breath and thank God again for delivering us safely.

At that moment, Dr. Patel, a young Indian resident who had been caring for Barry from the beginning of our stays in inpatient, stood by me. My anxiety was palpable. He told me that things did not look good, but Barry would bounce back. The slight Indian put his hand on my arm and squeezed ever so slightly. He and I had become friends in the course of our internment at St. Jude. Our conversations rarely veered from Barry's care, but when they did, we often talked about hope. On the dark, glassed-in corridor of St. Jude's seventh floor, I asked Dr. Patel why my God or his God would allow for such a thing as childhood cancer.

Our conversations often included the experience of suffering, evil, the role of God in the abyss of our suffering, and how we find hope again in our derailed, damaged lives. These conversations were essential to me as they were not only precursors for what my family would experience later in life, but they allowed us to put words and thoughts to what we were experiencing.

Dr. Patel and I discussed the possibility that God is willing to prevent evil but not able. If that is the case, He must be an impotent God. If He is able but not willing, He must be a malevolent God.

Dr. Patel thought that perhaps God is both able and willing but chooses to let things play out as they will. The doctor said we often don't know why suffering is a necessary component of human life, and we often don't get to know why. This troubles me deeply.

Later, I read the Apostle Paul's version of God in Romans 11:33–34: "Oh, the depth of the riches of the wisdom and knowledge of God! How unsearchable His judgments, and His paths beyond tracing out! Who has known the mind of the Lord? Or who has been His counselor?"

My take is that I cannot understand God. He is infinite and I am finite. Somehow, this thought has helped me answer the questions about suffering and evil; at least, it has helped diffuse my misgivings about my God.

Another time, Dr. Patel and I discussed Job and his willingness to follow God no matter what sorrow befell him or his house. I have read the book of Job several times and cannot come to grips with the story. My heart hurts so much for his losses. Yes, God replaced Job's family and gave him back more than he ever had. Was this good enough? I maintain that a loss can never be replaced. The damage and brokenness one suffers because of loss is so great that I cannot imagine being made whole.

Yet, something happens when we allow our minds and souls to accept the existence of God. Then we have the opportunity to hope, and it is in that hope that God exists.

After a long, sleepless night, Dr. Patel and I watched the sun come up over the Mississippi River. As the day wore on, Barry's staph infection began to respond to a new antibiotic cocktail that one of St. Jude's pharmacists created for him. As a matter of fact, a picture of Barry and me is in a pharmaceutical book that was published the following year.

By the weekend, Barry was feeling much better. Along with several male nurses, he watched the Oakland A's play a baseball game on TV. Barry knew everything about the A's organization, including Jose Canseco, Mark McGwire, Rickey Henderson, and the rest. He loved talking baseball with Ronnie, the nurse practitioner for C Section.

The following week, we were sent home again for a few days. Before we left the hospital, the intercom called Barry to C Section with instructions to come without his mother. This was curious, as he had never been called to C Section in this manner.

When we reached the waiting room, Mrs. Crawford from the Make-A-Wish Foundation approached us again. She asked me to go get a cup of coffee in the cafeteria because she would like to discuss some things with Barry. I was hesitant to leave them, but I decided a cup of coffee would do me good.

About twenty minutes later, the two found me and announced that they had come up with the perfect Make-A-Wish for Barry. Apparently, they talked about baseball and found they had much in common. Mrs. Crawford, too, was a baseball aficionado, so they got on famously.

"Barry and I have decided that he should go see the Oakland A's play and meet his favorite player, Jose Canseco," she smiled. "I'm leaving to get right on getting his wish fulfilled, and I'll be in touch later."

I was dumbfounded. A four-year-old and a sixty-something-year-old made plans without me!

So it came to pass. We were given plane tickets for the whole family, a hotel room, a meal stipend, and transportation. Our trip was planned for one week around the Fourth of July 1990 in Milwaukee, Wisconsin. The A's and the Milwaukee Brewers would face each other at the Brewers' stadium, and Barry would be in the middle of it all. Our excitement grew as we got closer to go-time.

From the plane ride to the limousine ride to the game, everything was wondrous! On the Fourth of July, a limo arrived in front of the hotel along with a motorcycle police escort. The boys' eyes were flashing with excitement, and for just a minute, our lives seemed almost normal. At the stadium, some friends who had previously worked with Brian at United Foods and now lived in Milwaukee provided a tailgate party.

As the game time drew close, we headed for our seats, which were directly behind the A's dugout. Before the game started, we were taken into the dugout for Barry to meet these athletic hulks. His idol, Jose Canseco, picked him up and walked him through the dugout to meet the other players. He put Barry down, and Mark McGwire played ball with him, as did Rickey Henderson. The men were so generous and loving. We were in awe that they showed such kindness to a little guy from Jackson, Tennessee.

Barry threw out the game ball before the game began. A mascot took Barry to the pitcher's mound, handed him a baseball, and instructed him to throw it to one of the A's players. At that moment, the big screen showed my little bald boy winding up for the throw of his life. The fans applauded; Brian and I cried; Ben was in charge of filming with the camera but forgot to turn it on; and Brad was to get Barry from the mound.

After Barry threw the game ball, he headed for the A's dugout, believing he would play this game with them. We finally got him to his seat behind the dugout by tempting him with a hot dog and a drink.

The game proceeded. Unfortunately, when Jose struck out, Barry was unhappy. He took his little glove and quickly climbed onto the roof of the dugout. Brian got him before he got too far. Apparently, Barry believed it was his turn after Canseco. After all, somebody had to hit the ball.

The next day, we went to another game hosted by the Brewers. Barry and the rest of us were taken to the Brewers' dugout, where he met Robin Yount, the Brewers' premier player. Yount presented Barry with the bat he had used in the game the previous day and signed it. Barry took everything in stride and acted as though he belonged to these athletes and their organizations.

Following the game, we were taken to a nearby tall bank building, where a dinner was set up on the roof so we could see the fireworks over Lake Michigan. We were hungry and looked forward to the fireworks display.

The elevators took us to the top of the building, but there was a set of stairs to climb to get to the roof. I was carrying my purse, the cumbersome movie camera, and a bag filled with family necessities when my sandal caught on the lip of one stair. I flew forward, bracing myself for impact and trying to protect the movie camera, which was not mine. In that awkward moment, I landed peculiarly. At first, I did not think I had hurt myself, but in short order, the pain from my wrist bolted through my arm. I knew I had broken my arm or wrist. What a mess!

Without blinking an eye, the police gathered me in a car and took me to a nearby hospital. There, my arm was put into a cast up to my elbow. I was given some pain meds, and another police car whisked me back through the crowds of people watching the fireworks. I got to see the tail end of the display.

The next morning, a friend from Jackson called me to ask how my arm was. I was puzzled that she knew about my accident. Apparently, I made the Associated Press wire that resulted in a blurb in the *Jackson Sun* describing my fiasco!

Our stay in Milwaukee was astounding. Among the other activities that Make-A-Wish planned for us were a yacht trip on Lake Michigan, where the captain let Barry steer for a bit; a meeting with the mayor, who gave Barry a key to the city; a trip to the zoo and botanical garden; and a royal send-off.

We were truly treated like royalty the whole time we were in Milwaukee. I thank the Make-A-Wish Foundation, Mrs. Crawford, the A's and Brewers, and the City of Milwaukee for making this trip one of the most memorable times of our lives. We are forever grateful to everyone who made a young boy's wish come true.

Chapter 10

Remission

I n June 1990, we drove from Jackson to Memphis and back, two hours round trip, for Barry to receive three minutes of radiation to his abdomen. The Ethel to my Lucy and her sweet three-year-old daughter, Hannah, accompanied us to Memphis most days. I appreciated their company, as two hours of driving daily quickly became tedious. The kids also kept each other company, so that made the drive easier.

When we got to St. Jude, Hannah often led the way and announced to anybody who would listen, "This is my boyfriend, even though he doesn't have any hair!" She sometimes allowed Barry to hold her hand on the way to the radiation department.

On the last day of radiation, Ronnie, our nurse practitioner, brought us more paperwork to sign. I thought I had signed every possible paper that St. Jude's lawyers could create, but more always seemed to be at the ready. Of course, we were told to return for a follow-up in three months, which made our departure more palpable. Still, the thought of cutting the umbilical cord to St. Jude and its people caused me great sorrow. Yes, I should have been jumping for joy that Barry was declared in remission, and I certainly was glad, but the security blanket that St. Jude provided was hard to leave behind.

We walked around the hospital to say goodbye to people we would not see for a while. We went to the gift store, where the sweet clerk always had a kind word for us, and bought some celebratory candy. At the end of the hall stood Danny Thomas's bronze statue on a pedestal. For the whole year we were at St. Jude, I had walked past this statue, each time rubbing Danny's proboscis, which had been rubbed to a bright, golden sheen by the many patients and families who wanted some "good luck."

Our final stop was to see Dr. Garcia in C Section, but he was out of town. As I looked at the familiar gleaming hallway and the doors through which we entered to begin the cancer journey, I recalled the excruciating screams of Barry and the other St. Jude babies who had to withstand spinal taps without anesthesia. A shiver ran through me to which I physically reacted.

I also remembered meeting George H. W. and Barbara Bush in the same hallway in 1989. When the president of the United States knelt before my ill child, I cried. Danny Thomas and the head of the hospital, Dr. Simone, accompanied the president and first lady as they made their way to other patients waiting to meet them. It was a special moment.

More memories flooded my mind until I finally said that we should leave.

I cried most of the way home, but Ethel and I talked about what we had to do next. Her glass is always full; her willingness to listen is always available. As we drove home, I began to make plans for the next installment of our lives.

A few weeks at home put us into a routine that all seemed to accept: Dad went to work; the boys enjoyed the rest of summer; Grandma cooked dinner; and Barry and I played. Even though life took on a semblance of normalcy, the whole time I was waiting for the shoe to drop because remission may only be short term. We learned to live each day and be grateful for it.

One evening, Brian announced at dinner that United Foods had given him six weeks to find another job. He plopped that piece of information into the middle of the dining table, and we looked at it like it was a foul-smelling piece of meat on a platter. How could they do such a thing? They had been so generous with giving time to Brian when he needed it and once even offered their private plane if we needed to transport Barry.

How was this possible? Apparently, the insurance that United Foods had doled out over the course of Barry's treatment at St. Jude far exceeded the amount they were willing to pay for a family. Instead of waiting for a relapse, they opted to release Brian on a high note when his son was deemed well.

As the Godfather often said, "It's just business."

Of course, they did not consider that we had three mouths to feed besides ours and Grandma's, and we did need a place to live. This maintenance costs money. What were we to do when both of us were unemployed?

Sleepless nights ensued again. I decided that I would go back to work earlier than I had intended, but that would not solve our problem because the private school for which I worked did not offer insurance or enough money for us to live. Since teaching was all I could think of doing, I decided to return to that school, and somehow, we would make do with the help of God. We had made it this far: Our child was alive, and our family was intact! However, I did start thinking about getting a teaching position with the public schools as the salary was much higher, and, at the time, they offered free insurance.

While Brian rewrote his resume and started sending letters of inquiry all over the United States, I began applying with the Jackson-Madison County School System and other systems in the area. Because the economic situation in the early '90s was tenuous at best, Brian received many letters of regret. He became somewhat despondent. How could a guy with a master's degree in business and experience not find a job? Months went by without so much as a bite.

One day, Ethel came by with a newspaper clipping that announced the opening of casinos in Tunica, Mississippi. The casinos had all kinds of job openings, including accountants. Even though Tunica was two hours from Jackson, we thought these jobs were worth a look. In Tunica, a human resources person told Brian if he became a dealer, his salary would far exceed an accountant's salary. Besides better money, he would receive his meals for free; insurance was applicable; and he would only need a dealer's uniform. Never in a million years did I think that I would be married to a riverboat gambler!

While Brian began working at the Hollywood Casino, I continued to search for a teaching position. The stars must have aligned because I received a call from the Jackson-Madison County School System wanting me to help design and write a new middle school foreign language program and then teach that program at Tigrett Middle School. I immediately accepted the offer, and our imminent fall into the poorhouse was avoided.

Brian was not paid right away because he had to complete dealer training, but he was employed in short order. His stint in the casino was to be short term until something better came along. It turned out to be an eleven-year stint that required a four-hour daily commute. He would leave at eight in the morning and return at ten in the evening.

Brian's job took a major toll on our family, and like the proverbial elephant, I haven't forgotten that he left me to tend to three growing teenage boys basically by myself. Yes, the money was good, but I did not like being a single mother for the week. Besides, he lost out on many of the boys' life events that he would never be able to regain.

Over the next ten years, the Fowler family moved forward. Even though Barry had lost the upper range of his hearing because of the cisplatin he received, he thrived in school. Ben and Brad also seemed to be doing well. I confess that I began to believe nothing else would harm us after we had survived a monumental life event in Barry's cancer treatment. Surely, no other tragedy would befall us. Little did I know that our cancer year was simply a precursor of what was to come.

This picture was taken at Olan Mills on the Saturday before
Barry entered St. Jude Children's Research Hospital in Memphis.

ABOVE: Brad and Danny Thomas in St. Jude's cafeteria.
AT LEFT: A St. Jude photographer took this photo of Barry to be used for my speaking engagements.

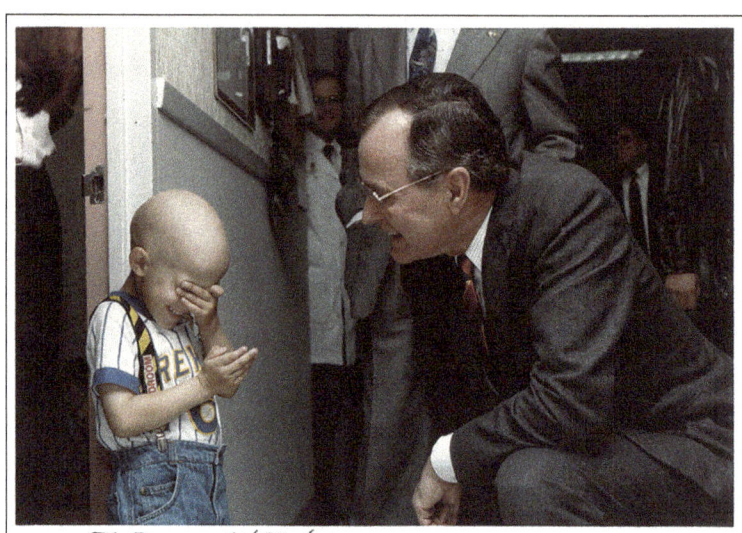

To Barrymore Zeb Fowler
With best wishes, *Geo. Bush*

ABOVE: President George. H. W. Bush spoke to Barry during a visit to St. Jude Children's Research Hospital in 1989. RIGHT: First Lady Barbara Bush sent this letter to us after the visit.

THE WHITE HOUSE

February 5, 1990

Dear Mrs. Fowler,

Thank you for your very kind letter and the photographs of George with your son, Barry, at St. Jude. George is a very caring man and I know his visit with the children meant a great deal to him.

Please know that your family will be in our thoughts and prayers.

Warmly,

Barbara Bush

Mrs. Barbara Fowler
105 Channing Way
Jackson, Tennessee 38301

George told me about Barry.
He loved him. God bless him.

Jose Canseco, Brian, and Barry in the Oakland A's locker room on July Fourth during the Make-A-Wish trip to Milwaukee.

Brad and I celebrated Christmas vacation in the snow in 1989.

Dr. Amar Gajjar was instrumental in working with Barry while we were at St. Jude. His friendship has been invaluable.

East and West Germans at the Brandenburg Gate in Berlin in 1989.

Barry and Dr. Victor Santana from St. Jude Children's Research Hospital in October 2025. After thirty-seven years, Barry met with Dr. Santana to thank him for all he did when Barry was a patient at St. Jude.

Brad's graduation portrait.

Rick Dacus took this photo in June 2004 and inserted an old photo of Brad into it so that I could have a picture showing all of us at age eighteen and older.

David, our guiding angel in Mexico, and Brian in front of the chapel in Acapulco.

Chapter 11

Lamentations

N ot long after our departure from St. Jude, Alexander and Olga returned to Russia. Our return to normalcy compared to theirs was very different. On June 6, 1990, Olga wrote me a letter that one of her colleagues sent to me from the United States as this colleague replaced her as a researcher at the University of Tennessee research labs. Both Olga and her husband are doctors; he was the head of hematology at a lab in Leningrad, and she was a research fellow in the same lab. The following is a glimpse of their life experience, as compared to ours. (I kept the grammatical and spelling errors to maintain the integrity of the letter.)

> "Finally we are home. Alexander is delighted to be with his loveling father and brother. My husband has a vacation now and spends his time

with Alexander. They have a lots of things to do. I started my work without any problems. The only problem is the absolute absence of any interest to my work in my mind. But I hope I will be able to restore my interest in future. I need to work to keep my mind bisy and to keep my salary. It is absolutely impossible to leave for one salary only. Our life in Russia changed crucially during this year. All stores are absolutely empty. Everything is a big problem, including very simple things necessary for life. Thanks God. I can use some things for Alexander and me which I took with me from Memphis. I was very clever. My husband is helping me getting a food from different stores. At daytime they are walking from one store to another. So my refrigerator is full now.

"I'm trying not to think about future and to enjoy every day of life when Alexander is in good health.

"In contrast to economical disaster, a political life is very interesting. A lots of new parties and groups, and lots of points of view. Sometimes is extremely difficult to understand who is right and who is wrong.

"We have even monarchists waiting for new 'tsar.' But I think it will be very difficult to find somebody who wants to be a tsar in this destroyed country."

Alexander was in remission for about six months before he relapsed. Again, Olga and Alexander made the long trip from Leningrad to Memphis. She told me that Alexander would need a bone marrow transplant if he was to have any chance at survival.

When Alexander was in remission, his bone marrow was extracted and frozen, as was Barry's, in the event a bone marrow transplant was necessary.

The idea behind the transplant is to kill all diseased cells in the body, along with all good cells, and introduce the new, "clean" blood stem cells, which travel to the bone marrow, where they are to produce new blood cells and promote growth of new marrow. Unfortunately, in Alexander's case, the procedure caused his death.

We visited with Olga and her husband at their hotel after Alexander's burial in Memorial Park Cemetery on Poplar Avenue in Memphis. Through glassy-eyed looks at us, she proclaimed, "There really isn't a God."

Her statement resonated with me again in October 1999. We were looking forward to fall break, as it had been a strenuous school year. Barry was looking forward to having a few days off to play; Ben was home from the Air Force and working nights; and Brad was commuting to Jackson State Community College from home. I was looking forward to taking a long nap before helping Grandma with dinner.

Barry, fourteen and in the eighth grade, asked if he could play football at North Side High School's football field with his three buddies. He said our neighbor Cal would drive them up and back. I acquiesced because I wanted my nap, but I told him they would have to be back by six for supper.

In retrospect, I wish I had not given in so easily and had said I would take him and pick him up. But that did not happen.

The ringing phone brought me out of my nap.

"Mrs. Fowler, you need to come to the corner of Oil Well Road and Steeplechase's entrance. There's been an accident," Cal said quickly.

Oh, my God! No!

I flew out of the house, screaming at Grandma, Ben, and Brad, "Barry's been in an accident!"

Approximately five blocks from our house, my child was crushed in the tuna can of Cal's car. When I arrived at that now infamous corner, an ambulance, multiple police cars, a fire engine, and people were already milling about the two crashed vehicles. The jaws of life were prying Cal's car open, and inside lay my unconscious child.

Apparently, Ben and Brad had been right behind me in Brad's car. Ben told me that I kept screaming Barry's name, trying to will him to come to. I remember wanting to help remove him from the wreckage, but I was held back by someone. *God, how could this be?*

The ambulance took Barry away; Cal, the other two boys, and everyone present watched the red lights of the ambulance disappear onto the US 45 Bypass. Immediately, Brad and Ben drove me to the hospital.

Someone had also called Ethel, and she met us at the emergency room entrance. Once I was with Barry in the emergency room, I held his hand and voiced like a mantra, "Please don't leave me. Please don't die. Please don't leave me. Please don't die . . ."

Someone also called Brian, who was working in Mississippi, to come home. I don't know how much time passed while we were in the emergency room until Brian's arrival, but it must have been at least two hours.

I hovered over Barry as the doctor and nurses worked to stabilize him. Then, Dr. Schneider, our friend and fellow church member, arrived. He took my arm and whispered that I had the right to have Barry airlifted to Le Bonheur Children's Hospital in Memphis. He recommended that I do this because Le Bonheur was better equipped to handle children than Jackson General.

At that moment, I thought that God was looking out for Barry. I learned later that Dr. Schneider's wife had seen the accident happen as their house was right across the street from the accident. She immediately called Dr. Schneider, who was on his way home from the hospital but turned around to meet us in the emergency room. Without his intervention, it would never have occurred to me to ask that Barry be flown to Le Bonheur to be treated. I felt some relief upon hearing that an airlift was a possibility because we had already had a positive experience with Le Bonheur ages ago.

Dr. Schneider re-explained to us that Barry had a very bad concussion and most likely a traumatic brain injury. No one could tell us how long he would be in a coma or what damage had been done to his brain.

The police report indicated Cal's car was hit on the side where Barry was sitting. The impact caused Barry to fly around the car's cabin. The report also stated that had Barry been wearing a seat belt, he most likely would have died. One of Barry's friends, Terry, a large, older boy, sat in the back seat with him and cushioned Barry's blow to his body. Apparently, Barry was jettisoned into Terry's ribs and broke four of them. Terry's injury was the only harm done besides Barry's head injury.

How could everyone else walk away from the accident, including the driver and passengers of the car that hit them? The police report also indicated that the other driver had borrowed the car from someone and did not have a driver's license. We never heard a word from them.

After Barry was stabilized in the emergency room, Brian and I escorted our comatose son to the hospital's helicopter launch pad. We had to drive ourselves to Memphis as protocol only allowed the patient and medical personnel to fly in the helicopter. As I watched the helicopter fly away into the dark sky, I prayed that God take care of them and bring them safely to their destination, but most of all, I asked God to bring Barry back to us. Standing on the dark roof, looking at the few stars that were visible, I felt that God had shut the door on us. *How could He let this happen to Barry of all the people in the world?! WHY, GOD? WHY?*

On the way to Memphis, Brian and I hardly spoke. What was

there to say? One of the things I have always loved about Brian is that he is a man of few words. I, the woman of many words, probably make up considerably for his lack of words. During this ride, even I had nothing to say. I could not wrap my head around the events of the past few hours, and yes, I was preparing to blame God for everything—no, not blame; hate is probably the more accurate word.

A doctor was already working on Barry when we arrived in Le Bonheur's emergency room. When we entered the room, the doctor said he needed me to hold my son securely while he drilled a hole into Barry's cranium to release the pressure that had built up in his skull. It is very hard to understand someone when he tells you that you are to watch a strange man drill a hole into your child's head.

I asked, "Won't he scream?"

He said, "I doubt Barry will, but I think you might."

He smiled at me and explained how I should hold Barry.

Having something to do helped, but when the doctor brought out a drill, I admit I wanted to stop him. Within minutes, he had created the hole, bandaged Barry, and had the nurse prepare him for his bed space. I asked what the next steps for Barry's recovery would be. The doctor said they would monitor his vitals, feed him intravenously, and wait. We would all wait.

Chapter 12

The Waiting Game

Wait. Wait. Wait. I hate waiting for anything! This time, waiting became the hardest thing I was expected to do in my life. My anxiety made waiting for Barry's recovery even harder. I wanted him to have a shot, get up, and leave with us to resume our fall break. That was not going to happen.

I began to think about waiting.

What is wrong with waiting? The old adage that "good things happen to those who wait" certainly became an adage because it smacked of truth. Optimists wait for their "ship to come in." Children wait for their birthdays and other holidays or in long lines at theme parks. We wait in line for a seat in a good restaurant or to see a good movie. Believers wait for the coming of Christ.

Waiting does often result in good outcomes; however, waiting for Barry to emerge from his coma left me feeling fearful, anxious, helpless, and apprehensive. Would Barry be a vegetable, totally bound to a bed or wheelchair? Would he ever recognize anything of his old life? How would, we, his parents and family, deal with a disabled child?

This was a different situation from cancer because the doctors thought Barry would come out of his coma, but they did not know what his personality would be like or what he would be capable of doing.

The reason waiting has always seemed so painful to me is because I inevitably choose to focus on that which would cause pain. I made myself crazy running through the possible scenarios. At some point while I was sitting next to Barry's bed and holding his hand, my mental fog began to clear.

I decided I needed to do the same thing that I had done when Barry had cancer. I dedicated myself to learning as much as I could about neuroblastoma then, and now I would learn as much as I could about comas and traumatic brain injuries. My resolution to learn kept the annoying waiting hours at bay and made me feel more able to handle Barry's needs once he emerged from the coma.

My self-tutorial began when Dr. Anderson dropped by and said she thought she remembered us from our 1989 visit to Le Bohneur. She was no longer a resident but was a full-fledged doctor. After I told her about my decision to learn as much about comas as I could, she said she would gather materials for me, and if I had questions, she would be more than happy to answer them. All I had to do was call her on her pager.

The next day, my literature arrived and I began to learn. Comas have four stages: unresponsive, early response, agitated and confused, and higher-level response. I concentrated on everything there was to read about Stage One. "The reader was to speak to the patient and assume he understands what you are saying; he was to tell the patient stories of the past; he was to allow visitors to speak to the patient without other distractions like the TV; he was to read to the patient; he was to show pictures to the patient and tell him what was on the pictures." And so I went about the business of following as many of the suggestions in the Stage One chapter of one book as I could.

First, I called home and asked the boys to gather certain titles, especially C. S. Lewis's *The Lion, the Witch, and the Wardrobe*; Barry's baseball cards from his current favorite baseball team, the Atlanta Braves; his immense book of collected baseball cards; and paper and crayons. Brian brought these items to me after he went home to take a good shower and pack a bag for him and for me, as we were now staying in Barry's room at Le Bonheur. We did not have to sleep in a motel as we did during our cancer days. Today, the Ronald McDonald House, the Target House, and a few other places in Memphis provide a home away from home for those of us who have to stay with our children in the hospital.

The night that Brian returned with all our paraphernalia, I took a long shower. Afterward, I sat next to him on the bed in the cold, utilitarian, brown-paneled parent room. I looked around and felt overwhelmed by our situation again. Brian never liked it when I cried because I'm supposed to be strong and in control. At that moment, though, I felt no strength, no control. My hair was dripping and soaking wet because the towel had fallen off my head. Tears and dripping water melded together to produce a wet towel.

Brian asked, "What's the matter?"

"What's the matter!" I responded. "Are we ever going to have sex again?" As quirky and odd as the question may seem, it was my way of asking if our marriage could stand this second catastrophe. I wanted to hear that he loved me. I told him I loved him more than ever for his steady, true manner. He folded me in his arms, and we cried together.

The statistics of failed marriages in the US are huge (almost

60 percent as of 2021), and most of these divorces do not have a catastrophically ill child or possibly disabled child in the mix. I read or heard somewhere that if a family has a catastrophically ill or disabled child, the divorce rate spikes from the norm by 10–15 percent, depending on the study.

One reason Brian and I are together is because we have loved each other since we were fifteen. We did not have our first child until I was twenty-nine, so we had many years together before we took the leap into parenthood.

Given what has happened to our children, our older parenting age was probably a good thing. Perhaps, our advanced child-rearing age allowed us to handle what was coming with some maturity, although I confess that sometimes I wished I could turn back the clock and start again.

I wanted answers to my questions: why were we chosen by Fate, by God, to endure so much tragedy, and why has Barry had to suffer so much? I'm not going to talk about what is fair because I don't think there is such a thing as fairness. But why was Barry dealt such an unfair hand? I've been told that the answer to my question probably would not satisfy me because I would still think he got a rotten deal in life. I have been told repeatedly that we don't understand God's ways but that He will lead us "through the valley of the shadow of death." Please, let it be so.

For the next few days, I spent ten to twelve hours reading to Barry, enlightening myself about comas and traumatic brain injuries, or holding his hand in between nurse and doctor visits. As before at St. Jude, I added a great number of new words to Barbara's lexicon at Le Bonheur: anticonvulsant, ventricular drain, electroencephalograph, angiogram, edema, and so on. I also showed pictures to Barry of our family and friends and talked until I was hoarse.

On October 23, 1999, the World Series began. I told everybody on the floor what a devoted baseball fan Barry was and invited people to come watch the game with us. I asked that they talk to Barry as well while they were with us. All kinds of people from the hospital stopped by for a few minutes or a few innings. Some brought snacks or drinks. We even sang during the seventh-inning stretch.

A festive atmosphere permeated the room during the games. Laughter or groans were often heard when a player made a bad play. There were cheers, especially when the Braves made a good play. All the while, like the elephant in the room, Barry, small and pale, lay on that hospital bed, not moving or uttering a sound.

The last game of the World Series and the last World Series of the millennium took place at Yankee Stadium in New York. The showdown was between the Yankees and the Atlanta Braves. Many of the fans at the hospital took bets for a quarter; most believed the Yankees would win because of their history. They were in search of their third world championship in four years. The Yankees were aiming to complete their first back-to-back sweep since 1977–1978; whereas, the Braves were trying to avoid losing their fourth World Series of the decade.

The last game was about to begin. Several people drew up chairs to the TV to get ready for the last spectacle. Before the game started, I asked Barry, "Which team do you want to win, the Yankees or the Braves?" No sooner had I finished the question than Barry ever so slightly raised his hand and made a tomahawk movement!

I screamed; everyone around us screamed. I kissed Barry over and over again. He was returning to us. People came running from all directions. Dr. Anderson hugged Barry, then me. The 1999 World Series finale was, without doubt, almost the most joyous ballgame I ever saw.

For the rest of that night, I held Barry's hand and could feel the wiggling of one or two fingers. Again, I was on my knees thanking God for His mercy on us!

Chapter 13

Rehabilitation

On November 3, 1999, Le Bonheur discharged Barry. He was transported to HealthSouth Rehabilitation Hospital in Memphis, across from Methodist Hospital on Union Avenue.

The discharge paper read: "The patient is a thin, white male child who is alert, restless, and nonverbal. He will follow some commands. Pupils are equal and reactive to light and some accommodation with extra ocular movements intact, bilaterally cranial nerves intact. Lungs clear. Heart has regular rate and rhythm. He grasps with the left hand and moves vs. gravity. Right extremity has some proximal motion and very little distal motion. Right lower extremity has antigravity strength and ROM. Left lower extremity has good strength and ROM."

I had a wheelbarrow of papers to sign before discharge, and Barry was prepared for the ambulance ride from Le Bonheur to

HealthSouth. Once he was installed in his new room across from the main nurses station, I prepared our next "home" for who knew how long. At HealthSouth, parents were allowed to spend the night in the same room as the patient, which made Brian's commute to Mississippi easier. Instead of driving four hours a day, his traveling time was cut down to two hours daily.

On weekends, Brian went home to wash laundry and bring back fresh clothes. Additionally, he went home to check on the builders. A few weeks before Barry's accident, we had contracted a builder to put an addition onto our house because our sons were large boys, and we needed more room for them and us. Having Barry in the hospital and needing to make decisions about the building added more stress to our already stressful life. The only good thing was that Ben had enrolled at Lambuth University in Jackson and lived at home as well as Brad. The two tried to help oversee what strangers were doing to our house.

Dr. Norstrom was the first doctor we met at HealthSouth and would be in charge of Barry's rehabilitation program. Then came a long line of extraordinary nurses, insurance people with more paperwork, physical therapists, occupational therapists, music therapists, speech therapists, and social workers. All proffered their goals for Barry and explained how each goal would be achieved. The sheer number of people interested in helping my child recover was breathtaking. I took notes so that I would be prepared for what was to come, and I would be able to tell Brian, the boys, Grandma, and friends the latest events in Barry's healing process.

Barry's rehabilitation began the very next day. He underwent a rigorous regimen of physical therapy and occupational therapy daily. His therapies took about four to six hours each day. When we had time off, I would read to him or take him for walks around the hospital in a padded wheelchair if the weather was pretty.

The nurses and I stuffed pillows and extra blankets into the wheelchair around Barry and propped his head up in a makeshift sling so he could see straight ahead. I looked forward to this time daily because I was so tired of sitting in a hospital room that even going in circles was exciting. I think Barry enjoyed the walks as well because I took sweet ice pops with me that he could suck.

As we circled the front of the hospital, we drove past massive planters, each filled with a gay array of colorful pansies. I told Barry to pick one bloom each day so that we could press them and put them in his scrapbook as a reminder of the many days at HealthSouth. Since he was nonverbal and had difficulty moving anything, I did the picking. Sometimes, if I chose a pansy he did not like, he groaned slightly until I showed him one that he liked. This gave me joy as I realized that he understood quite a bit but hadn't found his voice yet.

After one of our outside trips, Barry was scheduled to go to another therapy rather than take a nap. The physical therapist, Nancy, took him to a large room where physical therapies were performed at the end of the hall from his room. She placed him on a table and began to gently stretch his legs and feet because his ankles wanted to extend and point straight down. He slept in splints that kept his ankles straight through the night. Even after we returned home, he had to sleep in the splints to prevent his feet from contracting again.

Nancy's stretching exercises proved to be uncomfortable for Barry. After the leg and ankle exercises, she proceeded to stretch his shoulders, arms, and wrists. In one move, our sweet, petite Nancy stretched Barry's arm over her shoulder so that she had a better grasp of it. Apparently, Barry did not like this move and bit her hard in her shoulder. She screamed; another PT released Barry's teeth from Nancy's shoulder.

I grabbed Barry and hauled him back to his room. I told him that I felt like giving him a whipping, TBI or not. My voice was very loud because the desk nurse came in to see what the ruckus was about. I told her that Barry and I were having a "come to

Jesus" meeting because I was not going to tolerate such boorish behavior. I told him that if a therapist did something he did not like or if something hurt him, he should raise his index finger. We practiced raising his index finger for the rest of the day.

That worked because I frequently saw a raised index finger, especially when I wanted him to do something. By this time, Barry had entered Stage Three, agitated and confused, on the coma scale. On the one hand, that was good; on the other hand, we had so much to relearn that I could not see straight.

Each day, the therapists required Barry to do something new. I watched as he spent time picking up beans, coins, or blocks to transfer them into a receptacle. Sometimes he became agitated when his fingers couldn't pick up a block, so he threw it across the room. Of course, this could not be tolerated and required more meetings of the minds.

On most days, he was asked to stand for several minutes. That progressed to taking a few steps while holding onto two bars, and finally a belt was tied around his waist as the therapist guided him down the hall. On other days, he was taken to aqua therapy.

When Barry slept, he was zipped into a rope/cage to prevent him from accidentally falling out of the bed. One day, he had finished aqua therapy and was particularly tired. While he rested, I decided to cross the glass bridge between HealthSouth and Methodist to get a meal in Methodist's cafeteria.

Most of the time, I ate from the vending machines in the hospital lobby or whatever Brian brought. I thought I would have a good hour to enjoy a change of venue before Barry awakened. I even did a little shopping in Methodist's gift store.

At the end of the hour, I returned to our room to find Barry scrambling over his bed, his diaper torn to shreds, and diaper pieces decked the floor like leftover cotton pieces in a cotton field. When he saw me, he yelled, "No!"

This was the first word that he had spoken since the accident. I was so happy that I cried, unzipped him from his cage, and wanted to hold him, but he would have none of it. He was so angry and frustrated because I had left him that he hit me hard in the face. Again, we had to discuss means of handling himself when he was angry. One of the more difficult skills that TBI patients must learn is how to control their anger. We worked long and hard to modify Barry's behavior. Once in a while, especially when he is tired, he reverts to his initial bad behavior even today.

During November 1999, we had quite a few visitors. Among them were Reverend Irving and a church member named Laurie. I was in a place where life was pressing in on me again when they arrived on a dreary November day. They had been at a presbytery meeting in Memphis and decided to stop for a visit. I was so grateful to see these two people. They reached out to us with prayer and made sure we received cards from the church members and many, many prayers. The church, they told me, was at the ready to help us in any way; all we had to do was ask. Their kindness and generosity caused me to pause. Having visitors made me realize that we were not the center of the universe and that I had to make a concerted effort to shift my focus. Yes, of course, Barry was important, but as Dr. Abraham taught me so long ago at The Peabody, life is going on all around us.

Although Reverend Irving and Laurie did not stay long, they left me with some important things to think about. I poured my heart out to them: my hatred for Cal; my hatred for God; and my inability to forgive them both. Reverend Irving and Laurie listened to my litany of complaints and advised that I should rethink our situation totally. I should not only forgive Cal, but I should forgive myself. They saw me shifting the blame of our problems onto others as though that could make things better. They left me with a verse from Ephesians 4:32, "Be kind to one another, tenderhearted, forgiving one another, as God in Christ forgave you," and with a prayer that God would ease my heavy heart.

After they left, I thought that I did believe in forgiving others for their human wrongdoing; however, I had an incredibly hard time forgiving Cal. I had also lashed myself because I allowed Barry to take that fateful ride to the football field. Had I only driven Barry myself and picked him up, the whole outcome could have been different. Logic tells me that all kinds of things could happen even if I had delivered Barry to North Side and picked him up. So why was I yet harboring so much anger?

The visit that helped answer my previous question came one evening. Barry and I were watching TV when a soft knock on the door got my attention. I cracked the door and saw Cal and his family standing somberly in the hall. I stepped out hesitantly when Cal's mother asked if Cal could see Barry alone. Cal's head hung down onto his chest, and I could tell that he needed to ask Barry to forgive him for being the one to cause him so much suffering. I nodded and opened the door for him.

We all stood silently in the hall while Cal paid a kind of penance in Barry's room. Cal's family are devout adherents to the Catholic faith that made them pray to God and every saint for Barry's speedy recovery. Out of the corner of my eye, I saw Cal's mom praying on her rosary in her purse.

After a while, Cal emerged, red-eyed, from the room and whispered, "I'm so sorry." In that moment, I knew I had to work on forgiving Cal and myself. I did not want to be a prisoner of my own hatred. I did not believe Barry's circumstances were God's fault either. Forgiving is not about getting an apology or a show of remorse from the wrongdoer. It is about letting go of the pain and suffering we feel so we can be at peace with our lot in life and thank God that He walks with us.

After I saw Cal's anguished face, I knew he was suffering and would carry a trunkful of anguish for the rest of his life over the accident. Neither he nor I were looking for any reconciliation. We wanted forgiveness.

After Cal and his family left, I was reminded of Charles Dickens's *A Christmas Carol* where the ghost of Marley says, "I wear the chain I forged in life. . . . I made it link by link, and yard by yard; I girded it on of my own free will, and of my own free will I wore it."

Their visit and my subsequent thinking about forgiveness relieved me somewhat, but neither they nor any forgiveness would change Barry's condition.

One of the last events at HealthSouth affirmed that although Barry was damaged, he would regain much of his normal function and quite a bit of his mental acuity. Our morning ritual was to have Barry do as many of his care activities by himself, such as combing his hair and brushing his teeth. I usually helped him get dressed and tied his shoes or buttoned a shirt. Small motor skills eluded him and sometimes still cause him problems today. One morning near the end of our stay at HealthSouth, Barry wanted to try tying his shoes himself but was unsuccessful. That same afternoon, he tied his shoes perfectly. We were astounded!

Because Barry had reached Stage Four on the coma scale, the doctors deemed him ready to be released. Our last day at HealthSouth was December 3, 1999.

Chapter 14

Our Personal Field of Dreams

B arry and I stayed at home for the rest of December because we were given many instructions and many appointments with therapists in Jackson. We needed to address Barry's double vision, another of his health issues as a result of the accident. Because of his head trauma, the nerves and muscles that hold the eyes in alignment, also called "eye teaming," were damaged, resulting in double vision. We were advised to see an eye doctor in Memphis and begin the process of preparing for eye surgery. Our doctor recommended that we wait a while for the eye surgery because he wanted Barry to improve more physically and mentally.

In January 2000, Barry and I returned to Tigrett Middle School to finish the year. I was so grateful to the teachers, staff, students, and parents for taking care of Barry for the last five months of the school year. He could not perform many of the tasks taking place in his classes, but I could see that he was progressing rapidly. At the end of eighth grade, he even took a girl to the prom.

Barry wanted to play baseball again that summer as he had since he was five years old. At first, we were told that he would not be eligible to play because of the myriad of health issues afflicting him. I begged the Dixie Youth leaders to please let him play even if all he did was put on a uniform and warm the bench.

After hearing everything that Barry had suffered, coaches met with us and decided he would join the Crane Services team with Mr. Tandy, his coach. Since Jackson is a small town and because I've taught school here for so many years, people knew of Barry and his struggles. The coaches and players were apprised of Barry being on Crane Services and agreed to let him play at least once each game. Barry was not particularly happy, but we said he should thank God he was able to stand, run, and play. Our conversations about how glad he should be and how much worse his situation could have been usually calmed him enough to accept our reasoning.

As the season progressed, Barry played sometimes once and sometimes twice in a game and always struck out. In 2000, Crane Services had a pretty good team that allowed them to play in the championship. The last game of the season looked bleak for the team. The parents screamed for their boys to pull them through, but player after player struck out. As I recall, the score by the last inning was 1–0 in favor of the other team.

During the games, I usually sat in the bleachers with a cup of coffee and piles of papers to grade. I would look up periodically, but I figured I didn't have a dog in this race. How wrong I was!

Someone alerted me that Barry was in the batter's circle. Our team had two men on base, and we were one run behind in the bottom of the ninth. Why Barry was put in next still puzzles me, but I didn't worry because he was going to strike out. Perhaps the coach thought that the runners could make it to second and third, respectively, and the batter after Barry would bring at least one in. In any event, Barry, with a black patch over one eye so that he would not see double, went up to the plate. I noticed that instead of batting right-handed, he opted to bat left-handed. To this day, we have no idea why he chose to change things. The dread in the stands and in the many folding chairs behind the batter's box was a palpable, collective inhale from the fans. I don't think anyone breathed out on that humid night at Oakfield.

The first ball went by. *Strike!* Barry whiffed the second ball. *Stirrrike!* The third ball came rather slowly, and Barry connected. The ball went between third base and the shortstop. The shortstop had trouble getting it in his glove, and by the time he threw it to the catcher, the runner on third made it home. Because the catcher couldn't catch the ball the shortstop threw, the other runner made it home, too. Barry stood tall on first base, grinning from ear to ear.

The crowd erupted in a din rivaled in any baseball stadium in the world. The boys and coaches picked Barry up on their shoulders and marched him around the field screaming, yelling, and jumping full of joy.

Barry was responsible for winning the championship. I was screaming and crying; my school papers flew all over the bleachers as though they had wings. I didn't care, for my son got to experience what it means to be an MVP. Every now and then, I meet someone in Walmart who was present on that magical night, and invariably, we relive the moment Barry and the team had a wish fulfilled.

As was usually the case, summer passed too quickly. Barry enrolled at Jackson Central-Merry High School for ninth grade rather than North Side High School, where his brothers had attended. Riding with me to Tigrett daily, taking the bus to JCM from Tigrett, and returning home with me was easier than having him attend North Side; besides, most of the kids he knew were going to JCM.

Barry had always been a tenacious student, but schoolwork was more difficult for him now. For the next four years, he and I would sit side by side at the dining room table working: he on his assignments; me on grading papers. We often sat for hours because he was not going to bed until he had done everything his teachers asked him to do.

The TBI had changed him. As I mentioned before, Barry's frustration doing assignments that used to be easy presented a problem now. He often made a scene when it came to assignments in math, the most frustrating of all his subjects. I finally asked my neighbor, a math tutor, to work with him in all the high school math courses. Barry knew not to cause a scene with the tutor because he would leave, and then where would Barry be?

I also hired a Lambuth University student to work on science and history lessons with him. We went to see the Lambuth student twice weekly with Barry's assignments for the two subjects. I handled English and Spanish with Barry. And so we worked through his high school career. All that work paid off in the end because he passed his ACT with a 19 and was accepted to Union University provisionally. He even received an honors cord at graduation. We could not have been more proud of him.

As his high school years proceeded, Barry intuitively knew that he was different. His speech, hearing, small stature, and mental struggles all set him apart. High school kids are notoriously judgmental. They want nothing more than to be different from the herd, but when it comes down to it, they want to be exactly like their clique. Once accepted into some group, they can be cruel.

In ninth grade, Barry often came home sullen because someone made fun of him. He said he didn't have any friends because they laughed at him for his speech and stupidity.

Again, we talked things out and prayed. He got through his high school years with the help of Doc Needy, our church's youth group, former Mayor Bob Conger, our friends, and many other people. I was getting frustrated myself, having to talk to him so much daily while also taking care of everything at home and at school. I decided to find someone in whom he could confide.

Barry's sessions with Doc Needy were good for all of us. He kept notes during the week in a small tablet about things he wanted to discuss with Doc and found Doc's advice to be very helpful. Even Barry's anger and temper tantrums subsided while under Doc's care. I have found that a total stranger is sometimes far easier to talk to than a close friend.

Our youth minister was instrumental in explaining God's Word to Barry so that he could understand what the Bible was trying to say. He was also happy when he went on excursions with church, especially to summer retreats in Montreat, North Carolina, because he finally felt he was part of something where he was accepted. To this day, if you ask Barry how he has navigated the turbulent waters of his life, he always points heavenward and says, "It's all because of God!"

Without question, Barry has been an inspiration to me and others for his unwavering faith. In fact, he told me that God spoke to him in the hospital and said, "Everything will be okay." He believes in God with all his being; who am I to say it isn't so?

Bob Conger, Jackson's former mayor and a member of our church, took Barry under his wing. We had a program called Cow and Calf where an adult mentors a teen. Bob was a unique man whose humor and kindness toward Barry will always be in my heart. He often called us, and when I answered the phone, he would say, "This is Bob Conger. Can Barry come out and play?"

The retired Bob did not wish to have a conversation with me. He wanted to pick Barry up, play tennis with him, have some "buddy time," and return him home. I will always be grateful to him for caring about Barry.

In his second year of high school, Barry took Driver's Ed. Like all teenage boys, he wanted a "fine" ride. I had no idea where this "fine" ride was coming from because we were barely able to meet our expenses. He was sure he would be the recipient of a "fine" car soon.

In November 2001, we went before Judge Melrose for a settlement conference. Some time earlier, I met Dona, a lawyer whose three children I had taught, in Walmart and asked if she would represent Barry. She agreed and completed the necessary paperwork to present to Judge Melrose. She also asked if Jane, another lawyer and a friend, could act as guardian ad litem in our case. I knew Jane would make sure that any settlement made would be in Barry's best interests.

After the necessary procedures were completed and over $50,000 in expenses was paid, Judge Melrose called Barry to the bench because Barry asked if he could speak with him. Barry asked if he could spend some of the money to buy a car. The judge agreed. Barry was on cloud nine and gave me an "I told you so" look.

Judge Melrose also told us that if we agreed and signed off on everything that was presented that day, we could not come back for additional money. In other words, this would be a done deal. Had I known what the future held, I don't think I would have so readily assented. We wanted to move on with our lives, so we agreed.

In due time, Barry and I bought a used 1998 black Ford Explorer from a lot on Airways Boulevard. That purchase did more to boost his confidence than anybody or anything else. He also underwent successful eye surgery to align his eyes, but then he needed glasses. He was glad to ditch the pirate look but not too sure about being a "four eyes" now.

Although Barry could not play baseball for JCM, the tennis coach willingly added him to JCM's tennis team. Barry loved being an athlete and wore his tennis shirt proudly. The coach made sure he played every time, and his teammates treated him well, accepting him as a member of the team. I was grateful to them, too.

Barry's first three high school years flew by, but in 2004, his senior year, the unthinkable happened.

Chapter 15

Kiawah

For approximately seven years, four of my friends, known as the Divas, made the thirteen-hour trek to Kiawah Island off the coast of South Carolina, where Sue owned a vacation home. She invited us for several reasons, but mainly she felt we could use a change of venue from our everyday lives.

Of course, my family was not thrilled that I left them for a week in the summer, but I felt the need to head for the ocean with my friends to hit the reset button of my life so I could return to them refreshed and ready to tackle another year. Sometimes I think I was selfish for taking "me" time every year; yet, at other times, I was glad I could take advantage of Sue's generous offer.

Kiawah is one of those places that you see touted in expensive magazines. A concerted effort has been made by the builders of Kiawah to find a balance between nature and human intrusion.

My first time to visit this paradise left me speechless. I had never seen such natural beauty. Marshes, live oaks hung with Spanish moss, windswept dunes, lagoons, and wildlife—from dolphins to egrets to herons to protected loggerhead turtles—abound on the island. Miles and miles of beach run along the outskirts of the island, and, of course, the ever-changing ocean complements the pristine landscape.

I came to this natural retreat to be refreshed. As a child, I had never been to the ocean, but once I saw it as an adult, I fell in love. When I considered the ocean's allure, I thought it made sense that humans were drawn to it because we are approximately 70 percent water ourselves.

Whenever I went into the ocean, I felt like I was in the womb again. The gentle rocking of the waves, the tide rolling in and out in perfect rhythm, the sand cushioning the soles of my feet, and the sun kissing my upturned face all contributed to my sense of well-being. The power of the seawater washed and baptized me simultaneously. The intersection of sea, earth, and sky made me feel the presence of God like no other place.

Most mornings, one or all of us would walk miles along the beach. Sometimes we would sit and read or laugh about nothing; at other times, we were on a mission to hunt for the treasure trove of seashells. When rain kept us from the beach, we would ride our bicycles on the canopied trails of the island, enjoying the light mist that would leave us dripping wet. The camaraderie and friendships that were forged while in this most spiritual place will always remain with me.

Brian, Barry, and all of our friends returned to Kiawah once more in the summer of 2004. This visit turned out to be the most important of the trips because Brian and I had to reinvent the wheel of our lives here. No other place on earth could have guided us besides the magic of Kiawah Island, with the sea and the presence of God.

Rachel Carson wrote in *The Sea Around Us*: "For all at last return to the sea—to Oceanus, the ocean river, like the ever-flowing stream of time, the beginning and the end."

Chapter 16

The Night the Music Died

E aster 2004 was the last time that our immediate family spent together. Brad had come home from Middle Tennessee State University earlier in the week for spring break. He, Barry, and I attended Easter services together. Barry drove himself to church earlier because he was a greeter at one of the church doors, and he did not like to be late. I asked Brad to pick me up under the portico after church as I had volunteered to deliver several Easter lilies to people in nursing homes. We usually sat in the church balcony because we were often late and because I liked sitting with the teens. I felt more comfortable with them than I did with the adults in the sanctuary pews below.

After the service, I spoke to a few people and located the lilies I was to deliver. Brad was not under the portico and was nowhere to be found. I became irritated that he had opted to do something else instead of what I asked of him. Because I was now thinking of finishing our dinner and delivering the lilies, I wanted to get going. I found Barry and explained the situation. He and I prepared to leave when Brad drove up, asking where I had been. I told him to go home, and we'd see him after our deliveries. I was annoyed.

When we got home, I felt miffed but went to work on Easter dinner. That year, the holiday tradition had lost some of its luster because Grandma died in 2003 and we all felt her absence. None of the hustle and bustle that she exuded was present: no hot cross buns made from scratch, no homemade strawberry creme pie, no scalloped potatoes, and no other surprise delectables she could conjure in the kitchen.

My job had always been to set a beautiful table with my mother's lace tablecloth, using our best china and silverware. Grandma also always insisted that each of us choose one of the English bone china teacups, saucers, and dessert plates she had collected for us. Our grown men put up with the delicate china depicting dainty lilies of the valley, violets, or sprigs of lavender touching the rim of a plate. The boys groused at having to drink from these delicate cups, but they acquiesced because they knew the china brought her joy. No matter what misery had befallen us in the past, when a holiday came, she wanted tradition. In retrospect, I think she was right to hold on to times that represented happier moments.

Without Grandma in the kitchen this year, I was to take over our traditions, but I lacked enthusiasm. Because we missed her terribly, our dinner was a lackluster affair. Even though we had similar foods and table settings, everything was off—off by a lot. I usually said grace, which Ben and Dad tolerated and which Barry and I believed was as much of our tradition as everything else. We ate, but we ate with a kind of "let's hurry this up" attitude.

After dinner, I was doing schoolwork on the computer when Brad emerged from his room to hand me a paper that indicated he had received a small scholarship from the education department.

Usually, I would have made a big deal out of his success, but this time, I was too wrapped up in what I had to do and held onto some of my earlier annoyance. As he walked past me, I saw his disappointment that I was not impressed. He said he was leaving for Knoxville to spend the rest of his vacation with Annie, his girlfriend.

Brad was out of the house before I could kiss him goodbye or give him my usual list of dos and don'ts. I watched through the front storm door as he maneuvered his baby-blue, 1983 Cadillac Coupe down the street. Brad's choice of car had something to do with cost, but I think it had more to do with his sense of artistry. He liked everything to have style and be out of the ordinary.

When Brad was younger, he insisted on picking out wallpaper for his room. He wanted wallpaper like the paper he saw at Michael's mom's house. The background was white with black geometric lines forming the pattern. The ladies in the higher-end furniture store where we searched for that definitive paper raised their styled eyebrows when Brad described what he wanted. A middle-schooler did not often come to them with such a request. We did find the exact wallpaper, and I installed it in his room. He was pleased, and I admit that it was stylish.

After Brad left for Knoxville, I went about my business with only an occasional thought to his welfare; he was, after all, almost twenty-four.

On Friday night, April 15, 2004, I had showered and prepared to go to bed when the phone rang. By then, I had learned that when someone called late at night, it usually meant trouble. Brad's girlfriend, Annie, in a voice that was near panic, said we should come immediately because Brad was on the way to a hospital. Apparently, he had passed out and had a very weak pulse. A police officer then took the phone and explained that the ambulance was taking Brad to the nearest hospital, and we should go there.

My heart and mind went into overdrive. I told Brian to get out of bed and to get dressed now because Brad needed us. I threw on something and told Ben to stay with Barry and man the phone. We were on our way in minutes to make the five-hour trip to Knoxville. I was in full-blown anxiety, but I kept telling myself that God would carry us through this horror as he had on previous occasions.

Alternating from fervent prayers to immediate panic to a crying jag to prayer again, we drove through the thickness of the night. The road did not zip by as on other occasions but stood still in the black night. On both sides of the road, the trees stood tall and dark like attending soldiers. The occasional headlights from another car glared at us but were gone as quickly as they appeared. I whispered and choked out, "Through the valley of death. . . ."

All the while, Brian kept saying, "He'll be all right."

My heart was pounding; my breathing was shallow.

In 2004, we had bought Brian a bag phone, one of the first mobile phones on the market, because we felt he was on the road for far too long each day without having access to someone if he needed help. We had not gone too far when the police called us. The officer informed us that the ambulance was taking Brad to Fort Sanders Regional Medical Center because it was closer than the previous hospital. The EMTs felt he needed hospital care faster as his vitals were steadily decreasing. *OH! GOD!! HELP!!!*

I screamed and told Brian to drive faster. He was already driving at a breakneck 90–95 mph, which was not his usual speed. He liked to do things by the law.

What law is there that says your children will suffer? That you will suffer? That when you follow the law, you will still suffer? That if you don't follow the law, you will suffer? The Bible tells us that we will suffer on this earth but that Jesus Christ will deliver us out of suffering and bring us into the light. On the night of April 15, I only saw darkness.

As we approached the outskirts of Nashville, the phone rang

again. Brian moved to answer, but I told him not to do it. Fear had totally overtaken me. Brian told me to answer the phone. Reluctantly, I took the phone off its receiver.

"Mrs. Fowler, are you there? Listen carefully. Move your vehicle to the side of the road," Dr. Grant said.

At first, I thought there was an outside chance that Dr. Grant, the attending, needed permission to perform some kind of surgery, but I knew. I screamed, "Nooo!!!"

We listened as she told us our son had died.

Then, there was nothing—only numbness. I seemed to go deaf. The only thing that interested me was a piece of paper caught at the base of the rail by the roadside that was attempting to free itself from the chicken-wire fence. No matter how hard the wind blew, the paper could find no escape—not at that moment.

In the darkness of the night, the doctor told us the most important information of our lives, and I did not understand a word. In retrospect, I was glad it was dark. I feared looking at Brian, dreading what I might see reflected in his eyes.

We drove the rest of the night in silence to Knoxville. I watched the yellow line of the road blur; nothing stirred me. We were both in shock! We had become two strangers occupying the same space, keeping our own counsel, trying to put the Humpty Dumpty of our lives together, and I was wondering where God was.

To this day, I do not know how Brian found the hospital where our son lay. The sky was beginning to lighten ever so slightly. Daylight and sunshine seemed unnecessary. I found comfort in the dark. The light would make me face a reality I was not prepared to handle.

Dr. Grant and two nurses met us at the front desk of the hospital and immediately ushered us into a consultation room. The doctor explained exactly what she had done to resuscitate Brad, but again I heard nothing she said. Yes, I heard the words, but I did not comprehend any of them. She finally wanted to know if we wanted to see him. *Yes, of course. No, if we see him, he'll be dead. Yes, I need to see if what you are saying is true. No, I cannot see my lifeless child.*

She asked again, but this time I asked her what she would do. She said she would not want to see him.

"I would want to remember my child living," she said.

Brian and I looked at each other, and I knew he agreed with Dr. Grant. I had to have proof. I told Brian that he did not have to go with me, but I had to see Brad myself. A nurse escorted me to the room where Brad lay on a tall bed.

We stopped in front of the door before she pushed it open. I slunk into the room to find a guard standing at the end of the bed and to see Brad high up with the IVs, ventilators, and resuscitation equipment around and on him. I touched his arm. It may have been cold, but I didn't know. At this point, I felt absolutely nothing!

Brian followed me to Brad's room, and I heard him crying. Those tears meant nothing to me. Nothing!

In the consultation room, we were given a plastic bag with Brad's belongings. I saw the keys to his Cadillac in the sack and remembered thinking that the most important thing was to get the Cadillac and take his car home because he would need it. That little bit of denial would flower to the size of an atom bomb.

We were told that Tennessee law required an autopsy for people under age twenty-five. This meant that Brad's body would remain in Knoxville for a few days until the autopsy could be performed, although I was ready to bring him to Jackson that night. Getting the autopsy results would require weeks.

We left with Brad's few belongings and decided to pick up the Cadillac at Annie's apartment. As we approached the door, I felt the early morning light encroaching around us, and the accompanying cold air penetrated me to the bone. I could not stop shivering. The cold was the only thing I felt. We didn't have to knock on the door because Annie was awaiting our arrival.

One light was on in her living room. She asked us to sit down and told us what happened that Friday night. I had never gotten a chance to speak much with Annie before because the few times she was in Jackson, Brad whisked her away before I could have a decent conversation with her. He was secretive about her, but mostly, I think, he was afraid I might embarrass him. Because I taught many of his school friends, he did not like bringing them home for fear I might say something untoward that would embarrass him or his friends. He didn't want to hear stories about my classes, even though he knew quite a bit. As he got older, his unfounded fear of being embarrassed abated.

In the early morning hours of April 16, Annie and Brad's parents got to know each other. She told us that her parents had taken Brad and her out to dinner. After dinner, Brad went with some friends to their friend Carl's apartment, where Annie planned to meet him after she changed. The group planned to hang out together before the last of the semester resumed. She said that Brad grew hot and went to the stairs to get some fresh air when he collapsed. One of the boys found him and alerted 911.

Annie told us that she and Brad began their relationship when he studied for a year at the University of Tennessee. Her father owned the apartment house where he lived. As she spoke through her tears, her mother entered the room from Annie's bedroom. Apparently, Annie wanted to talk to us alone about her love for Brad and the events of the night. I respected her for that. Before we left, we hugged and kissed each other. The realization that the loss of her first love would stay with her for the rest of her life made me even sadder. I was helpless to provide a contingency plan for her; we did not have one for ourselves either!

Brian suggested we get a cup of coffee at Shoney's before we headed home. By this time, I literally hurt all over, from my head to my toes. We drank the hot coffee, and I wondered if other people in the restaurant could see my pain. Brian and I sat in silence. What was there to say? What was there to do?

When we walked toward the Cadillac and our car, my legs began to shake. At the door of the Cadillac, I fell to the ground. I don't remember Brian picking me up; I don't remember driving our car home. I remember excruciating pain.

We never stopped driving until we got home and parked the cars in our driveway. I looked for the boys and found them sitting on the steps of the back porch. The sight of Ben, the hulk, and Barry, the mouse, sitting side by side opened the floodgates. My grief knew no bounds and had no end. The boys, Dad, and I held each other as though we were in a freefall that none of us knew how to stop.

Later in the day, Ethel told me that I had called her from the car very late, after she had gone to bed, and asked her to go to our house and tell the boys that Brad died. You can only ask a sister to do such a terrible thing. She spoke to Ben, and he did not want to tell Barry. Ethel said she didn't either and that it was his responsibility as Barry's older brother. She got into her car and drove to our house, but she waited in the driveway. She soon heard Barry yell; his voice was extremely loud.

After the outburst subsided, she entered the house to find the boys sitting on the couch together in shock. Their shock blossomed into a nightmare that was and still is palpable. The death of a sibling presents some serious problems to the remaining siblings. Ben found that he could not handle such profound loss, while Barry trusted in God so much that he became our inspiration and strength. He often admonished me, "Just trust God, Mom. He knows what He's doing."

Who can disavow such unwavering faith?

Chapter 17

A Funeral

I don't do funerals well. After the death of one of our own, we are forced to figure out who we are, what to do, and how to face a future without the one we loved. A friend said we had to make funeral arrangements. No, I was not making any arrangements, but deep down, I knew we were required to perform this unthinkable task for our son. In denial, I fought the reality of Brad's death.

The professionals of Arrington Funeral Directors in Jackson handled Brad's funeral arrangements as they did Grandma's. In retrospect, her death made Brad's arrangements easier because we told the director to make the same arrangements as they had for Grandma's funeral: a graveside service with a simple, closed coffin, and we would arrange for someone to say a few words.

Two thoughts struck me as we sat in the director's office, waiting for him to bring paperwork to be signed and for payment to be made. First, I was taken back to 1959, when my mother and I arrived in New York City from war-torn Germany. Second, why did I not want a funeral of pomp and circumstance celebrating Brad's life?

From NYC's immigration office, my mother and I were told to take a bus the next morning to Quincy, Massachusetts, where my aunt Xenia and uncle Ivan, who had sponsored us, lived. We would remain with them until my mother and I got our land legs.

After the immigration officials dismissed us, we walked a few blocks. We were told that we could find several hotels and motels close by where we could spend the night before completing the last leg of our journey to Massachusetts. My mother carried our one suitcase as we perused the block for a suitable resting spot.

With our earthly possessions in tow, we entered the quiet lobby of a white-columned house. I had never seen red carpeting before and thought I would like to have some in our home when we got to Quincy. A man in a suit greeted us and asked if he could assist us.

In her broken English, my mother asked, "How much one room for night?"

The man raised his eyebrows, but he understood what my mother meant and guided us in the right direction. Apparently, my mother mistook the funeral home for a bed and breakfast.

At age ten, I was no help, as I spoke no English and relied solely on my mother's directives. Two doors down from the funeral home was a small hotel where we spent our first night in America, the America of streets paved with gold!

While we waited for our funeral director to return with paperwork, I asked Brian if we should do more for Brad's funeral. Here, things got tricky. We were both in shock and in denial and were useless at making any sound decisions. I knew Brian wasn't going to offer any suggestions, so we went with what we had arranged for Grandma.

Even while making arrangements for Brad's interment, I

believed he would come back, and that thought was foremost in my mind, day and night. Stress does enormous damage to those undergoing the bereavement process, even if the one grieving outwardly appears to be in control. I wanted to sign the papers and get away from Arrington as quickly as I could.

When we arrived home, friends, church members, neighbors, and acquaintances brought food, gifts, and books dealing with grief. They came one after the other for over a week. I entertained each one on the back porch overlooking the lake if the weather permitted. I was grateful for the diversion they brought and thankful that they loved Brad and our family so much that they were willing to do the hard work of grieving with us. I don't intend this as a funny comment, but our porch became a kind of psychiatrist's couch. Here we could talk freely about Brad, and our visitors did not mind crying with us in the natural environment that surrounded us.

April 21, 2004, was a dismal, rainy day. We hoped that the rain would subside before the funeral, but Mother Nature did not comply. We had to move the service into the chapel on the grounds of Highland Memorial Gardens. I asked Ethel, Bud, and our college friends who had flown in from out of town to sit behind us for moral support. Debbie, Brian's sister, had also flown in from Rochester, New York. At one point before the funeral service, Ben pulled me aside and asked if Annie, Brad's girlfriend, could sit in the front with us. She and her family had come to pay their respects. Of course, Annie could sit with us. She embodied what could have been part of our future: a daughter-in-law and grandchildren.

To my amazement, the chapel was full of mourners. Arrington's directors told me later that they had to turn people away. I am grateful for each person who chose to send off Brad with so much love. I asked Barney, Brad's good friend and a burgeoning youth minister, to say a few words on Brad's behalf. I also asked my former headmaster, who was also a Methodist minister, to remember Brad in some way. My friend arranged for a member of her choir to sing "On Eagle's Wings" a cappella.

As Barney spoke about his dear friend, I absolutely fell to pieces. We all did. He asked those who loved Brad to lay hands on each other as he prayed. I do not recollect any one thing Barney said, but I felt the love Brad's friends had for him.

When the headmaster got up to speak, he said there was little he could add to what had already been said. However, he did remember Brad's beautiful blue eyes. He pointed his index and middle fingers to indicate how piercing Brad's look was. After that, I don't remember anything. My pain was increasing to a point where I thought I would pass out. I wanted nothing more than to be in the coffin as dead as Brad was.

When the headmaster prayed, I couldn't. As a matter of fact, I do not recall being able to pray at all for quite some time. Our God had abandoned us for reasons only He knew. My anger with God grew exponentially as each day passed. I also chose to blame God for Brad's death.

When the singer finished her song so powerfully, my heart became slightly hopeful. She sang the last verse of "On Eagle's Wings" with so much love in her voice that no one stirred in the chapel.

> And he will raise you up on eagle's wings,
> Bear you on the breath of dawn,
> Make you to shine like the sun
> And hold you in the palm of His hand.

As people approached us gingerly to give their condolences, I thanked each one. I also invited everyone to come to our house to celebrate Brad's life. One of my teacher friends had erected a tent in our backyard because it was raining and our house wasn't large enough to hold a big crowd. Some church members and friends organized food and drinks at our house for those who chose to spend more time with us. I knew this "party" was part of the protocol of funerals, but I wanted to crawl away and die.

Brian and I did not want to watch as the workers lowered Brad into the ground in the driving rain. My heart couldn't take any more. Later, my friend told me she stayed and watched as Brad was laid to rest.

When we arrived home, we saw many cars parked up and down the street in front of our house. I do not remember much about the rest of the day.

I kept remembering a call from the organ transplant organization. The woman had asked if I would consent to donate Brad's eyes. How could I even consider blinding him? He might need them to see—those blue eyes!

Even after his funeral, I kept thinking that I couldn't donate his eyes because he had to see. How could she call me?

I was reminded of "Buffalo Bill's," a poem by e e cummings that mentions blue eyes:

> and what i want to know is
> how do you like your blue-eyed boy
> Mister Death

Exhaustion, emotional overdrive, and several sleepless nights had finally taken their toll.

I was depleted, finished.

Chapter 18

They Came

The weeks after the funeral were a blur. One day moved into the next with seemingly little difference on my outlook or my relationship with God. If anything, God appeared to be very distant. As a matter of fact, everything I did, everyone I met, and even my family seemed to be far, far away.

My pain had not subsided; my wailing and keening continued throughout the nights. The emptiness in my being created an abyss that grew darker and larger with every moment's passing. The question I struggled with the most was: Why did God rescue Barry twice from Death's claws and took Brad so quickly, so easily? Why? Why? Why?

Visitors during the day gave us a diversion. We had many visitors, but a few stand out in my memory. On one of the first days after Brad's death, Steph, one of my students at Madison

Academic High School, arrived with a sack of Sonic burgers after her shift. She wore her uniform and Sonic's distinct smells from the kitchen. She plopped the sack into my arms and said, "I've got nothing else to give you, but I love you!" She hugged me hard, gave me a kiss, and ran from the door to her broken vehicle.

I watched her run and cried again. Steph's life had not been easy. She spent most of her last year in high school living out of her rundown car. What money she had, she had to spend on herself to keep her head above water; yet, in our time of sorrow, she found it in her to comfort and love me. What an extraordinary person!

Another visitor who helped bridge my out-of-control emotions was a man who sold us several cars over the years. As we sat on my patio couch, he told me about how he caused an accident many Christmases ago that changed him inexorably. His wife and unborn child died in the accident, but he and his son were left unscathed. They were on their way to have dinner at the grandparents' house.

We cried together as he peeled back the layers of his sorrow, grief, and guilt. I mention him because on the outside, he appears to be a jolly fellow without a care in the world; within, he carries so much pain. His advice was to seek professional help. He said that even now, when the memories flow into the forefront of his mind and depression holds the upper hand, he has a "lay down" on the couch of the professional who has helped him through the years.

I took Jack's advice and went to a psychiatrist. My main concern was that I would never stop crying. The psychiatrist advised me to cry, for tears are valuable; they are like a bridge that unites our inner and outer selves. They provide emotional release and thereby heal our emotional wounds. He explained that genuine tears give us permission to express our hurt. Further, the language of tears lets others come closer to us because they see that we are as vulnerable as they are. Our tears are also expressions of love.

The psychiatrist said that he would like to wait a while before he prescribed antidepressants so that I could undergo the initial phases of grief without medical interference.

In time, I tried different antidepressants until I found one I could tolerate. Taking a pill for my emotional state was foreign to me because I never liked taking as much as an aspirin, but dealing with pain that had cut so deeply into my mind and soul had never been part of my past experience. I had to try antidepressants if I were to function during the day. Eventually, pills did help keep my emotions in check so I could return to work.

Another memorable visit was from a parent whose children I've taught. He asked what he could get for me to help ease my pain. Tongue-in-cheek, I requested that he get Brad to give me a phone call. I know that sounds snippy, but I explained to him that a phone call from Brad, telling me that he was fine wherever he was, would release the vise grip that grief had on me. I knew my request was impossible, but that is what came out of my mouth.

A few weeks later, that same parent arrived on my doorstep with a gift. It was a replica of Britain's red telephone box. He said, "Keep this near so you can get Brad's call." I found his gift to be so touching—yes, I cried. To this day, the red telephone box sits on my desk, and I still expect that call.

As I had done with our previous life events, cancer and TBI, I decided to busy myself with the business of learning about grief and searching for the God who would not abandon us. Many friends brought books, articles, magazines, and church literature pertaining to grief and Compassionate Friends material. In time, I could focus on readings such as Rabbi Harold Kushner's *When Bad Things Happen to Good People*, Joan Didion's *The Year of Magical Thinking*, C. S. Lewis's *A Grief Observed*, and Barbara Rosof's *The Worst Loss*.

Although I now had a bookshelf full, not one book has been able to answer my questions. That does not mean that people who are in a state of grief should not read these books and articles;

rather, it means the reader should understand that not one will offer the answers for which he is searching. Yet, reading about other people's experiences with grief and with God can help bring one's own thoughts into perspective.

I finally turned to the Bible to find an answer. Remember that I was quite angry and frustrated that our perfect life had, in my estimation, turned out so imperfectly. My present semi-atheist self was angry with God for having allowed this tragedy to happen. My God was supposed to be able to beat evil into the ground with the flip of the wrist. The psalmist cried in Psalm 22:1–2:

> "My God, my God, why have you forsaken me?
> Why are you so far from helping me, from the words of my groaning?
> O, my God, I cry by day, but you do not answer;
> And by night, but find no rest."

Christ uttered the same words on the cross. Feeling abandoned by God, I had no more need for Christianity.

After studying Job multiple times, I saw someone like me who raised questions about God's role in human suffering. Job talked as though God had a split personality: the good God and the malicious God. In his initial days of grief, C. S. Lewis struggled with the thought that God might be a "Cosmic Sadist."

Job's story distresses me to this day. I do not and did not believe in a malicious God. Job suffered immensely since everything he had and everybody he loved was taken from him. He even suffered physically, but he seemed to want the God he had prior to his tragedies. Even his wife, who had suffered along with him, told him to "curse God and die."

Although Job and his friends thought God had abandoned him, Job held out hope. God later restored everything to Job and more. One of my issues with Job and God is at the point when Job's life was restored. So what? What about his previous family? Was he to pretend they never existed?

In the end, Job learned that he was never cut off from God: He could still experience God in the midst of suffering, even if he didn't understand why he had to suffer in the first place. I would not learn most of Job's lesson about God until much later.

Intervention 2

Hebrews 12:1-2

After the funeral, we were so despondent, unfocused, and unable to do much of anything that I could feel atrophy in all my limbs. Brian suggested we take a walk at Liberty Garden at the end of our street. I balked at the idea of moving even a little for fear of some other tragedy felling us. He insisted, and we walked in the park a little each day. In order not to cry during our walks, I counted steps. This mindless activity at least got my body to move. After a few days of walking, I looked forward to some physical activity.

My mother, who did not attend Brad's funeral, sent me a long letter from Pennsylvania, where she lived with her fifth husband. She decided not to come to Jackson for several reasons, not the least of which was her broken heart. She called Brad "Dooney" when he was younger. Her letter was full of memories of her grandson and full of so much sorrow. As an afterthought, she added a small slip of paper on which she wrote the words of Hebrews 12:1–2:

> "Therefore we also, since we are surrounded by so great a cloud of witnesses, let us lay aside every weight, and the sin which so easily ensnares us, and let us run with endurance the race that is set before us, looking onto Jesus, the author and finisher of our faith, who for the joy that was set before Him endured the cross, despising the shame, and has sat down at the right hand of the throne of God."

I taped that little slip of paper over my desk for inspiration.

Another Madison student, Christa, visited and presented me with a gift: a purple cross with the words of Hebrews 12:1–2 inscribed on it. It has been on my kitchen desk since she brought it to me. Not only do I remember her when I look at the little, purple cross, but I am reinforced daily by the strong words inscribed on it.

One day, I decided to take another walk in the park because I found that doing something and grieving was preferable to sitting and grieving. Brian and the others decided not to accompany me. As I made my way on the narrow, paved walkway through the park, I noticed I was the only one walking.

When I looked up from counting my steps, I saw a tall, black man walking over the expanse of lawn toward me from Serra Chevrolet. He was wearing a black T-shirt and black pants. His long strides and large body propelled him forward in my direction. I decided to keep up my step count and walk past him.

When he was within ten feet of me, he suddenly turned and slowed his gait. On the back of his T-shirt, in large, white letters, the words of Hebrews 12:1–2 astonished me. In the course of a few days, I saw these verses as if I needed to read them at least three times in order to comprehend what they meant.

The man and I walked in tandem for about five minutes. Then he began to run. I could see his back going around the bend and expected him to pass me shortly because he was running at a fairly quick pace.

By the time I reached the other side of the park where I could see most of the pathway, the man had disappeared, but the message on his shirt stayed with me: "Let us run with endurance the race that has been set before us."

As I continued walking, I was not only struck by the coincidence of seeing the Hebrews message again, but I felt God was telling me to get on with life. There was more to be done.

Intervention 3

Hi, Dad!

Brian lurched into the kitchen on one of the first nights after he went back to work, looking like he had seen a ghost. His sallow skin and the almost frightened look on his face told me something bad had happened. He said that around the Brownsville exit on Interstate 40, about thirty minutes from home, a car got into the lane in front of him and traveled with him until he reached Jackson.

At first, he said he didn't notice anything odd about the car because he was driving automatically, but then he looked at the license plate. It read, "HI, DAD"!

Brian was so startled by what he read that he almost lost control of the car.

I thought that was odd, too. We knew people had all kinds of things printed on their license plates, but we believed the "HI,

DAD" license plate was a message for Brian from Brad that he was okay. Some who read this may think it was a coincidence that Brian saw the words, but we believe the message was an intervention to help us along the long road of grieving.

Because I am a skeptic, I decided to Google several sites to see how many license plates have been issued with the words "HI, DAD." I could not find one state in any of the contiguous United States to sport such a plate.

Intervention 4

Acapulco

I n July 2004, Brian and I decided to take a trip to Acapulco, Mexico, that I had planned and paid for in January. We both felt a need to remove ourselves temporarily from everything that reminded us of the last few desperate months. During the same week, Barry went on a youth trip, and Ben stayed home to mind the house.

The diversion of the flight and arriving at a destination we had never visited proved to be a good idea. Brad's death was never far from our minds, but the trip gave us a little respite and helped us to compartmentalize our emotions.

The Qualton Club in Acapulco is an all-inclusive resort located in the center of Acapulco Bay. The resort was reasonably priced and catered primarily to tourists from Mexico City. We were among few Americans who vacationed there. I liked the resort immediately because I was able to be anonymous among the friendly, courteous locals.

Our room overlooked the turquoise bay. The horseshoe shape of the land allowed the waves to crash onto the shore with that rhythm of water I so love. Since there was no air-conditioning, we left the floor-to-ceiling glass doors open in our room day and night. The ocean breezes flowed over us with a gentleness that caressed our weakened constitutions.

Most of the time, the sheer curtains that hung over the doors billowed into the room, creating their own waves. The view from our little balcony and our bed was to the southern end of the horseshoe cliff, where an enormous white cross guarded the bay. Each night, the lighted cross was the last thing I saw. At this point, praying was problematic for me, but the sight of the cross did much to calm me and encouraged me to attempt a reasonable prayer.

The day after our arrival, we were scheduled to take a tour of Acapulco with other hotel guests. After an al fresco breakfast, we headed for the van. I thought we were early because no other guests were waiting. David, our driver and tour guide, invited us to get into the van because no one else would be joining us. That suited us fine. The van could hold about twenty people, and David was losing money with only us to tow around.

As he drove, David gave us much information about Acapulco and its history. Our first stop would be La Capilla de la Paz ("The Chapel of Peace"), which I saw every night from our room. The chapel overlooks Acapulco Bay from the southern end and offers the most beautiful views of the bay. The gardens around the chapel are lush and inviting for visitors to take a peaceful rest.

On the steep ride to the chapel, David told us its history. In 1967, two sons of a well-to-do family died in a plane crash. Parents Carlos and Milly Hauss decided to commemorate their sons by building a chapel on top of the cliff in the residential complex of Las Brisas. They not only wanted the memories of their sons to live on, but they wanted to inspire peace in a city that was very much troubled by violence. The chapel opened in 1971 and was ecumenical. Sculptor Claudio Favier donated his work, *The Hands of Brotherhood*, to be placed on the grounds of the chapel by the magnificent white cross. The brothers and their parents are buried at the chapel.

Of course, as David explained the family's story and the boys' death, I returned to our own grief and began to cry. David ceased his ongoing lecture, and we rode the rest of the way to the chapel in silence.

When we got out of the van, David said, "Take your time, Señora; we are in a place that will give you peace." He was so gentle and kind that I became even more emotional.

The cross, the sculpted hands, the open-air chapel, the story, and the beautiful scenery brought me to my knees. I prayed fervently, not in anger, not trying to make a deal, but for the first time in a long time, praying in hope and in gratitude.

After experiencing the peace of La Capilla de la Paz, we returned to the van for the rest of the tour. We saw the magnificent cliff divers, and our last stop was at the Silver Market in downtown Acapulco. We watched the traffic jams of the city, including the men on Coca-Cola trucks with rifles. Apparently, Coca-Cola was a prime commodity and often stolen.

We moved at a snail's pace. By this time, Brian and I had moved to the front of the van to be near David so we could ask questions and hear him better. I sat in the front seat overlooking shorter cars and motorized vehicles of all kinds. When we came to a complete stop, a small car edged in front of us. In large, white letters, the word "KORN" covered the dark back window. I inhaled unsteadily because Brad's favorite band was KORN.

Why would that car with "KORN" on it, much like Brian's "HI, DAD" experience, show up in front of us? Why in Acapulco? Was it a coincidence?

At that point, we told David of our trauma. He listened and acknowledged our pain with a calm demeanor that seemed like he had already been made privy to our troubles. When the tour ended and we returned to the resort, David took my hand, kissed it, and said it was a pleasure for him to be our guide.

When I read his business card, I saw his name was David Gabriel L. I believe David was sent to be our guardian angel on that day in Acapulco to help us on the long road of healing.

Chapter 19

Rescued

Returning home from Acapulco was a blessing because I realized how much my family needed me. The thoughts of suicide that I continued to entertain needed to stop. Even though I grieved profoundly, I knew my plan to die in Brad's Cadillac had to be canceled because of Ben.

Ben had turned to alcohol to ease his pain. While we were gone, he probably drank to excess often. Early one morning, I heard him stumbling about, moving things in his room loudly, and crying. I got up to see what he was doing. When he saw me, he ran out the door, holding an immense pile of clothing, all on hangers. I yelled, "What are you doing?"

I ran behind him in my rather short, shredded nightgown, but I didn't care. Ben got into Barry's Explorer and started the engine. He had not had time to shut the door when I lunged into his lap, probably mooning the neighborhood, and held on to the steering wheel with all my might.

He screamed, "Let go! I'm leaving!"

"Where are you going? Why?" I screamed at him.

In his slurred, drunken voice, Ben said he had killed a man, and he wasn't going to jail. He said he was sorry to steal Barry's car, but he had to get to Mexico pronto. He tried to pry my fingers off the steering wheel, but I held on tighter. At last, he succumbed to me and fell into a crying heap of sorrow.

Apparently, Ben had run into a tree, and his car exploded and burned. Luckily, he had gotten out and found his way home. Luckily, too, he did not kill a man, only his car.

When he was finally lucid, we talked. Losing his brother was too much for Ben. He said that life was not worth living and that he wanted out. It had not occurred to me that Ben was suffering as much as Brian and I were. I made a deal with him: I would not think of suicide anymore because I needed him, Barry, and Brian so, so much, if he would not consider doing harm to himself.

Our pact has held; however, I have often found it hard to adjust to Ben's life responses. He no longer believes in God. He hates much about the world. He does feel a great responsibility to take care of Barry and us. I am grateful for that, but I wish he had someone else to care for and love. I wish he had children, but he says he refuses to bring anyone into this "f****** world."

Selfishly, I would like a grandchild, but part of me agrees with him. The world is difficult and mean, and when tragedy and suffering happen in the life of someone you love, then the world and the good it has to offer is suspect.

Because we were so broken-hearted, Brian decided to bring a most wonderful life into our midst, a bichon frise that I named Fufu. This little dog did more to help me than any advice or pill. He was the runt of the litter. Wherever I went, I carried him in a plastic basket lined with a soft towel. He loved me unconditionally, and his sweet manner comforted me. I talked to him; I cried into his soft, curly hair; and I slept with him. He became like a life preserver that was always available. What a joy he was!

Brian became jealous of our relationship and decided he needed a sweet dog to love. A few weeks after Fufu's arrival, Brian brought another bichon frise that we named Fifi. Her temperament was totally different from Fufu's, but Brian loved her, and that is what mattered. Ben got himself a baby, a part pit bull named Kat, and Barry had his cat, Furby. These animals provided each of us with love and understanding that no human could ever supply.

When Brad's autopsy report finally arrived, I felt no closure. I read it many times. I did not understand how Brad died. His body was his temple. He took care of himself so well—he exercised, was careful about his eating habits, studied nutrition, and went for checkups with the doctor. As a matter of fact, he had a physical the month before his death. How could he die?

I called the pathologist responsible for the autopsy in order to get a better understanding about the cause of Brad's death. With the autopsy papers strewn before me, I listened as the pathologist walked me through the paperwork, explained about myocarditis, and explained the scars she found in the back of Brad's left ventricle. She was patient, but I didn't understand why he died. Why couldn't they keep him alive?

After I spoke with the pathologist, I did try to stop reconstructing his death every day and reinterpreting the autopsy report. Whatever took Brad's life will forever be a mystery to me. Yet, reading and rereading the report provided a physical explanation as to his absence in our lives.

I finished the last few weeks that remained of the 2004 spring semester. The students, faculty, and staff of Madison Academic and my close friends were instrumental in helping me each day. I realized how much more my students gave to me than I could ever give them. My love for even the most trying of them was immense. I viewed them as my children whom I had the privilege of escorting through a portion of their lives. For a long time, I have believed that the people with whom we come in contact were meant to be because our job was to learn from each other. I also told my students about my belief that life is the true school in which we learn.

Because I taught literature for the last thirteen years of my career, I was able to use the work of the best authors the world has produced to teach my students life lessons. What a privilege it has been to teach!

Teaching also gave me a chance to get away from the active business of grieving. The hours away from acute grief were like lily pads on the pond where I could think about something else, associate with everyone at school, and compartmentalize my hurt. Of course, summer would give me many free hours to grieve.

I spent a portion of each day at Brad's grave. As I sat on the marble bench that one of his friends supplied, I spoke to him often in anger. When I got tired of crying, I meandered past the other graves around Brad's. Grandma and Grandpa Fowler are buried a few rows away from Brad's grave. Three of my former students are also buried near him. Their deaths angered me as well: one by suicide, another in a drunken driving accident, and the last was murdered. All were younger than twenty at the time of their deaths. It may sound macabre, but walking through the graveyard gave me a sense of peace. That had not always been the case.

The new school year would begin in late August, and I found myself looking forward to teaching a new batch of teens. Barry would soon begin classes as a freshman at Union University, and Ben was working and trying to cultivate a relationship that would end in marriage.

Over the summer, Brian found an interest in ancestry.com. He would call me to see how many children this or that relative from the 1800s had and how many of those children died. I suspect his interest stemmed from trying to understand how his family and others navigated life when the unthinkable happened. Perhaps, he wanted to discover a history that would explain Brad's death. Often, he indicated that so-and-so died of a heart attack at a young age. Brian's father had succumbed to heart failure.

Brian's sudden interest in the past provided some concrete information around which he could wrap his mind and not feel so guilty. Whatever the reason for his interest, I am glad he found a way to distract himself from grieving all the time.

Thus, each of us started to ride on our newly created wheels as we headed into the future: Brian, Ben, and I back to work; Barry to college.

The next horror to come truly blindsided us and broke us completely.

Chapter 20

No Mercy

F all is not my favorite time of year anymore, but come to think of it, neither are any of the other seasons. In October, I was supposed to celebrate Brad's birthday, not remember Barry's near-death experience. Grief washes over me again every October until it drowns me every April.

The 2004 school year was already in full swing, and the students and I were preparing for another fall break. Barry was already home on fall break from Union University.

Ben was working nights and sleeping during the day. Two days before our fall break, he came home at six in the morning as Brian and I went out the door to go to work. By ten thirty, Barry had a death grip on Ben's arm and was complaining about an upset stomach and a terrible migraine. Ben told him to take the migraine/seizure medication that the doctor had prescribed the last time Ben took him to Regional Hospital after a seizure and then go to bed.

The first time Barry had a seizure, Ben threw Barry into his car, and, barefooted, he carried Barry through the emergency room at Regional without stopping at the front desk. Security and the front-desk operator ran after him as Ben bulldozed his way into the emergency room, carrying his unconscious brother. They immediately brought Barry to by giving him a shot of Valium and prescribing more medication. Thus, Ben telling Barry to go to bed with his medication was reasonable, and he promised to play a video game after Barry had slept.

Apparently, Barry chose not to go to bed but instead decided to fold the clean clothes that were strewn on my bed. Ben was awakened by the sound of something akin to an alarm, a low, buzzing sound. He checked on Barry and found him breathing raggedly and clutching a handful of laundry to his chest, wedged between the nightstand and the bed.

Ben picked up his rigid body and placed him on the bed. He attempted to straighten Barry's legs and arms but had no success. When Ben noticed Barry wasn't breathing, he flipped him on his side. Ben's 911 call was answered immediately because we live a few blocks from Regional Hospital.

The EMS shot Barry with Valium that released Barry's grip on the laundry and allowed him to be put on the stretcher; however, he did not regain consciousness. Barry was taken to Jackson-Madison County General Hospital and immediately installed in the ICU. Ben's quick action probably saved Barry's life. Dr. Barnheart determined that Barry suffered a grand mal seizure that resulted in another weeklong coma.

After the ambulance had taken Barry away, Ben called me. I was in the last block of the day when the secretary told me I had an important phone call that could not wait. Our procedure at school was that we would not take phone calls during class. Rather, the secretaries would leave a note about any phone calls we received, so I thought it strange that I was being called out of class. My steps quickened from the second floor to the office as I thought of the possibilities.

When I answered the phone and heard Ben's voice, I knew that something terrible had happened. I listened as he explained the situation. Since this was not my first rodeo with tragedy, I calmly told him to call Dad and send him to the hospital. I asked the secretary to get someone to cover my class, rushed upstairs to collect my belongings, and headed out the door to deal with another unthinkable loss.

Dr. Barnheart met us outside Barry's ICU room and painted a grim picture of the probable outcome of his coma. He intimated that a second coma always resulted in the loss of further mental and physical capabilities and that there was a chance Barry would be totally disabled and spend his days in a wheelchair.

At this point, I was able to take in Dr. Barnheart's information, but I told him that he did not know my tenacious son, who had withstood neuroblastoma, a TBI caused by a car wreck, and the loss of his middle brother earlier in the year, and was walking and succeeding in life. I don't think I had to tell him that Barry also had to deal with a noncompliant mother.

Dr. Barnheart was such a soft-spoken man that I wasn't sure he should be the one to oversee Barry's treatment. I soon discovered that Dr. Barnheart did not just cross his t's and dot his i's; he did so several times. He was at the hospital every day and sometimes twice, especially when Barry's kidneys started to fail and he had to have dialysis.

The grueling month we stayed at Jackson General was difficult in many ways. Once Barry came to, which we thought was miraculous, he continued to have a low-grade fever. No one seemed to know why. I spent most of the time with Barry when he was allowed to see a family member in the ICU. The rest of the time, I waited in the waiting room until it was time to go in and see him again.

Even though Barry was semi-conscious, he was not as responsive as he had been after the first coma. His eyes didn't seem to focus, and, of course, he was nonverbal.

One day, it occurred to me that the IV dressing on his arm looked as though it had not been changed for several days. Apparently, the nurses from one shift to the other thought the previous shift had taken care of the dressing change. I decided to peek under the dressing, and, to my alarm, I saw red streaks emanating from the IV site. Immediately, I called for a nurse.

The subsequent brouhaha was amazing! Doctors, nurses, blood techs, and administrators rushed to our room. Barry received antibiotics to kill the infection caused by the ICU nurses' oversight; administrators gave their apologies; and doctors who never saw Barry came in at all hours. It was quite a scene. He still has a scar on his arm where the infection was.

Once his infection cleared, Barry was transferred to a room in the physical therapy wing of the hospital. One more time, he had to relearn everything he had learned previously. He was not walking nor feeding himself. I also noticed that everything he tried to do was much more difficult for him now. Additionally, his frustration and temper were almost out of control. What a long road lay ahead of him and the rest of us! Our grief over Brad's loss was compounded by the results of the grand mal seizure.

After the first brain injury, Barry's personality had changed. He will tell you himself that he became a better person because he had a TBI. I am not sure he's right, but again, who am I to question how another person feels about himself? Yet, our rambunctious Barry had now become a more introverted person. I wondered what the outcome of this second brain injury would be. What kind of son would we have?

The weeks of therapy at Jackson General flew by. We were told that Barry needed to transition to another therapy hospital because he needed additional skills before he could safely go home. Thus, we were transferred to the rehabilitation unit of Sumner Regional Medical Center in Gallatin, Tennessee. Family was not allowed to stay with the patient during the week, but we could visit on the weekends.

The floor on which Barry was kept reminded me of a prison. Some very sick people with TBIs resided on this floor. I was sad to see so many suffering in their bodily shells and sad to see my son among them. Once again, I reverted to the "it's not fair" scenario that I had so often visited. Why had we been dealt such an unfair distribution of human suffering? Once, maybe; twice, okay; three times, too much; four times, no, we do not deserve this. But then I remembered Job's reasoning that we live in an unjust world in which fairness doesn't exist. I have worked hard not to expect anything to be fair but find myself resorting to the concept when I can't figure another way.

Barry spent approximately five months in Gallatin. In that time, he improved dramatically. He never returned to the Barry we had after the first TBI, but we had to live with a new Barry who would be permanently disabled, mentally and physically. The therapists worked to help him to walk, learn to care for himself, feed himself, and speak. His brain nerves had not yet re-circuited so that he could function more normally. He had frequent outbursts of "Meeeoww" at the most inappropriate times.

After a few months of hospital therapy, Barry was deemed advanced enough to move into an apartment with three others in a similar condition. Assistants lived with them 24/7 so that their clients could learn independent living, including self-care, grocery shopping, cooking, socializing, and working. Barry went to work at the local Walmart with a job coach in the afternoons, while mornings were taken up with physical or occupational therapy.

During the 2004 Christmas holiday, Barry was allowed to come home for a few days. What were we to do? I wanted Christmas to go away, but Brian insisted we celebrate with Barry and Ben. I said I would go through the motions of dinner, but I was not up to getting a Christmas tree. In the past, we had always made selecting a live tree from a lot a tradition. I was not going to select any tree or put up any lights and decorations. If Brian wanted a tree, he would have to get it and trim it.

Brian opted to put the lights on a twelve-foot fake tree we had, and he told me to put our Christmas decorations on it. I surrendered, took the top off the box that held many of the children's homemade ornaments, and collapsed onto the floor. I thought I had no more tears to shed; yet, there I was, a broken mother with a dead son and two broken sons.

Barry came to me and held me in his now-stiff, rigid way and kissed the top of my head. I pulled myself together because I had no right to cry. If anyone should cry, it was Barry. Not once has Barry blamed God, Cal, or anyone else for his situation. He is not happy about being disabled because his long-term memory allows him to recall what life was like before his TBI. He is often sad that friends he had in the past have moved on with their lives: They went to college, got married, have jobs, and are raising children. He wishes he could be on the same life path, but he says, "It wasn't meant to be."

Barry doesn't struggle with unfairness and God; his God is good and would not consider hurting anyone. I am learning to accept a God who is good and does not deal with the fairness or unfairness of the world. Barry is still teaching me.

As for the Christmas tree, I refused to put our old ornaments on the tree because they would be painful reminders of what we had lost. Instead, I had another idea: Barry and I would bake gingerbread cookies and hang them with red ribbons. We got busy and made more than seventy-five gingerbread dogs and cats. After we finished decorating the tree, we called Dad and Ben to have a look. Barry and I in unison shouted, "Christmas has gone to the dogs and cats!" And so, we celebrated Christmas dinner, now with two empty seats; yet, we celebrated because Barry was alive.

In late spring, a vocational rehab counselor suggested that Barry attend Tennessee Rehabilitation Center (TRC) in Smyrna, Tennessee. He would be enrolled in the TBI program that had recently been upgraded with a new facility and new programs. We prepared him to go to TRC as though he were attending college.

Ethel went with us to help move Barry into his room. She even taped a few posters on the walls of his room, telling him that all college kids had posters on their walls. Bless Ethel for her ever-optimistic view of life.

We made sure that the caretakers at TRC were aware of Barry's breakthrough seizures. We were assured that they would take good care of him. I called every night; however, I never got much out of him because he was working on putting thoughts together.

Every Friday through Sunday, we drove to Smyrna to be with Barry. We found a Presbyterian church to attend and tried to do activities Barry enjoyed.

A few weeks into the program, the TRC director called, said that Barry was not rehabilitated enough for the TBI program, and asked if he could be transferred to the vocational program. Essentially, he would learn how to do one activity for several hours a day, like piecework on a line in a factory, with other disabled people. The only requirement was that he must get along with others. Apparently, Barry did not like this transfer but was unable to verbalize his feelings. He ended up in a pushing match with another client that resulted in his ejection from TRC.

In retrospect, discontinuing at TRC was a good thing. We, including the vocational rehab counselor, had sent Barry off too soon. When I collected him from TRC to go home, I noticed he had not taken all his medication. I decided to stop at Starbucks to get Barry a frappe and me a coffee for the ride home. As I was about to turn into the driveway of Starbuck's, Barry had a seizure. It was late; I was alone with him and worried. I held him with the hope he would come out of it. He drooled, rolled his eyes, got stiff in his arms and legs, and eventually relaxed. I knew then it would not be long before he was back. These unannounced seizures were scary, but scarier yet was that the present meds were not controlling them well enough.

We were exhausted when we got home. From that day, Barry slept with me again so that I could be aware of any seizures he would have in his sleep. Of course, my sleep could hardly be called sleep because I felt the need to be on duty throughout the night. To this day, I sleep very little at night but take a long nap during the day when I know someone is with Barry.

I spent many hours over the next several days speaking with the vocational rehab counselor to determine our next strategy for Barry's treatment, therapies, and ways to improve his quality of life.

But before we would embark on a new venture, we would take a vacation in Panama City Beach, Florida. I needed my beloved ocean, and I needed to think.

Intervention 5

Anonymous Lifeline

The minute we arrived at the ocean in Panama City Beach, I threw open the sliding glass door to the balcony, looked over the gray-blue expanse of water and sky, and took the deepest breath I had taken in a long time. I wanted to take it all into my body to become one with the ocean and sky.

In *The Awakening*, Kate Chopin says, "The voice of the sea speaks to the soul."

The voice of God speaks to me when I am still and listen to the waves crashing on the shore. I asked that we be given help as we navigated the new waters of life with Barry. *Give us courage; give us strength; give us enough intelligence to do what is right for him.*

Day after sunny day, we walked the shore or sat in beach chairs, taking in the beauty before us. We took Barry into the calm waters and played and laughed. He was uncertain as the small waves covered him, but he soon acclimated to the rock 'n' roll. His skin took on a bronze glow, and his appetite improved. Everything improves by the sea!

One day, Dad and Barry decided to take a nap rather than go to the beach with me. The late afternoon, just before sunset, is one of my favorite times. Most beachgoers have gone, and the feeling of a day well spent finds its way into my thinking. As I was ruminating about this and that, a curly-headed, middle-aged woman and her friend sat in the empty chairs by me. We acknowledged each other, and Shelby offered me a glass of wine. The three of us chatted about the lovely time we had at the beach when the conversation turned more personal.

Shelby asked if I had come to the beach alone, and I told her that my husband and son were in the condo napping. She offered that she and her friend along with her disabled son decided to come to Panama City Beach from Dallas for a few days as the friend had rented the condo. When I asked about her son, Shelby said he had suffered a traumatic brain injury in a car accident a few years ago but was doing all right. He was in the condo watching television.

Of course, I perked up after I heard that our sons suffered a similar injury. We talked well into darkness. I told her that I would like her son and mine to meet. We arranged to be on the beach at the same time the next day and bring our sons.

I was excited for the boys to meet each other. Shelby's son was slightly older than Barry, but they got along fine. We talked about her son's therapies and treatments. When I told her about Barry's breakthrough seizures, she said that her son had them, too, and then she gave me names of the medications he was taking. In addition, I expressed my concern about taking Barry anywhere because of his unannounced seizures.

Shelby told me about a drug she didn't go anywhere without; it was called Diastat AcuDial, or diazepam rectal gel. She said she had to use it before on her son, and it worked like a charm.

We continued chatting for a bit longer, and she said that they had to pack as they were going home in the morning. We exchanged addresses and phone numbers and wished each other well. I felt such a kinship with her because we were able to share our pain with each other and knew that another understood.

The next summer, Barry wanted to go to Montreat's Presbyterian youth conference. I said he could go if I went with him because he wasn't strong enough, mentally and physically, for me to let him go, even with our church leaders. The session approved me to be a chaperone for the college kids and Barry. This was also the first year that the Montreat conference incorporated college-age kids into the program. Barry and I attended the classes deemed for the college kids.

Toward the end of the week, we were in the cafeteria line for dinner when Barry had a seizure. He was behind me because I was busy getting our plates arranged when one of the kids alerted me. Everyone in the cafeteria came to see what was happening. I asked one of the cafeteria workers to help me get Barry into a private place because I had to take off his pants in order to insert the diazepam capsule into his rectum. We pulled him into the kitchen while someone else called for an ambulance to come from Black Mountain, North Carolina.

Literally within a minute of inserting the drug, Barry was alert. I was so grateful that I had the medication with me. By the time the ambulance arrived, Barry was up and talking. The EMS workers checked his vitals, and when they were satisfied he was stable, they left.

The outpouring of sympathy for us from the kids was truly inspirational. Before his seizure, they ignored his presence, but afterward, they included him in their activities even if he couldn't participate properly.

After we got home from Montreat, I called Shelby in Dallas to thank her so much for the tip to get diazepam. However, I got a recording saying that the number I was calling had been disconnected. I thought that I had probably written her phone number incorrectly in my address book. Next, I wrote a letter to her explaining our Montreat adventure and thanking her for the drug information. Within a few weeks, the letter returned with a stamp indicating that no such address existed in Dallas. My curiosity was now piqued. Could I have gotten her address wrong, too?

I looked up Shelby's name in the Dallas phone book. Neither her name nor the address she gave me showed up in the phone book. Then, I called the Dallas County Courthouse, seeking help to find this mysterious woman. I explained why I needed to get her address. The lady at the courthouse was sympathetic and wanted to help me. She took the information I had and said she would call me back once she had some more information. Several hours later, she called and told me that no such street existed in Dallas, and she could find no trace of the woman's name.

I was stunned. My only response to meeting Shelby was that she was sent to me by God to help me with Barry. My belief in the miraculous continued. This intervention was the last one I experienced to this day.

Chapter 21

What Remains . . .

L ife events hold together and shape the intricate tapestry of a family's lives. The family members weave that tapestry made of threads from the support of the religious community and the friends who walk with the family through valleys of unspeakable grief and tragedy.

I would like to change the proverb "It takes a village to raise a child" to "It takes a village to support a family in times of sorrow." For the Fowlers, our various villages provided security, help, support, and love when we needed it most. We will never be able to repay them, but we have tried to help when others need our support.

After we returned from Panama City Beach, the vocational rehab counselor continued Barry's therapies at our local STAR Center, a nonprofit organization that helps persons with disabilities improve their physical and mental capabilities through technology, art and music therapy, vocational training, and job placement. Barry was not particularly happy about the hours of computer work he was assigned, but he did love music therapy. The STAR Center was important to Barry because it gave him purpose and hope. For four hours per day, he had a mission: to improve himself in any way he could.

One day, when I picked him up from the STAR Center, he handed me a piece of paper. He said he had written a song and that they had made a recording of it. I could hardly collect myself to drive us home after I read it. The following is the song my son wrote about his brother:

> "Oh, I hope you are having a good time in heaven.
> Oh, I miss you, but I hope you're having a good time up there.
> I am just thanking God every day for having me to be able to live each day healthily.
> You are resting in peace, thankfully.
> Now you don't have to worry about anything.
> But I will get a chance to see you again someday.
> You and I used to fight all the time but we worked out our problems.
> Oh, that's just part of growing up.
> We both tried to look and do our best in front of people.
> You are resting in peace, thankfully.
> Now you don't have to worry about anything.
> But I will get a chance to see you again someday."

Even after Barry had completed his programs and therapies at the STAR Center, Mr. Hardy gave him a job several days a week to shred papers or do other tasks that were needed. This was an important job because it allowed me to continue working, and I knew he was watched in case he had a seizure. Several of our church members were helpful during this period because they willingly picked Barry up in the morning to deliver him to the center. They continued their "taxi" service later as well. I will forever be indebted to them for their service.

I was able to return some service to the STAR Center by speaking at fundraisers, much as I had done for St. Jude. Keeping a nonprofit alive and healthy is quite a feat, but the STAR Center has managed to keep its head above water.

During this time of rehabilitation, I hired sitters when one of us was not able to be home with Barry. I tried about four different women until it became apparent that they would not work out. One of the women worked a night job and slept during the time she was supposed to watch and ensure Barry did not have a seizure. Another brought her grandchildren, who created havoc in the house and broke some of Barry's belongings. Another smoked, and that drove Barry crazy. The last one stole things.

I was at my wits' end. Brian and I decided that one of us had to quit work and stay with him. We decided that he was the more logical choice because he was getting tired of driving to Tunica daily anyway. Eventually, he got a job at Lowe's for the shift from late afternoon to closing. This way, Barry would never be alone. We even had most weekends together.

One Saturday morning, Dad was making pancakes, I was luxuriating with my cup of coffee, and Barry was reading my mother's large-print Bible. He was somewhere in Genesis with the goal of plowing through the whole Bible. We were comfortably sitting at the counter when Dad let out a scream, followed by a four-letter commentary addressed to the pan where he burned his finger. Without warning, Barry sent my mother's Bible, open to Genesis, sailing across the counter and slamming into Dad's back at the stove. In his robotic voice, he bellowed, "You need to read this!" Then he emerged from his chair and attacked Dad in the stiff manner of the brain-injured.

I spat out my coffee and yelled, "Barrymore Zeb Fowler, your mother is too old to get the belt and beat your sorry, little ass! I just want you to imagine that I'm doing it!"

Then the standoff between the two resulted in a laugh at me.

I knew that Barry's tirades were the result of his brain injury, but that did not make them easier to tolerate. I am grateful that Barry believes so strongly in God because God has helped him suffer through so many hard days. I'm equally glad that Barry has a dad who puts up with his daily outbursts without so much as lifting a finger against him. On the other hand, I often visualize me slapping him silly, but my love for my child is far greater than words can express, so hurting him in any way is impossible.

We have had other dinner, lunch, and breakfast conversations that would make the average family cringe. Early in his employment at Outback Steakhouse, Barry came home, seeming depressed, and was quiet during dinner. Evidently, a customer made fun of his voice and intimated he was retarded. Over our dinner of sweet potatoes and meatloaf, he told me quietly, "I'm going to kill myself."

"When are you planning this event?" I asked while chewing a piece of meatloaf. "Do you have a plan?"

"Not yet," he mumbled.

"Well, I suggest an accident on the interstate. You drive ninety miles an hour and hit an eighteen-wheeler of my choice—blue, I think. You have to promise to hit it on my side, hard, because I cannot live if you are dead. Okay?"

"Oh, Ma, you're nuts!" he said with a small smile.

I know I'm nuts. I know he means it. I also know if I give in, it's the end for all of us. Dinner continued with no more dysfunctional talk about suicides or accidents. When he felt the stupidity was over, Brian asked, "Got any dessert?"

Barry's work at Outback and the people who work there are wonderful, especially Marty, Barry's former boss. Without his job as greeter, I don't know what would have become of Barry. Yes, there were occasional customers who had little compassion for someone different from themselves, but most customers were nothing but kind. The job gave him purpose, confidence, and a sense of independence he would otherwise not have had. I am extremely grateful to the Outback staff for their support and willingness to employ Barry.

Along with our church members, STAR Center's staff, Outback's staff, Madison Academic High School's students and staff, and many of our friends, we moved forward in life and joined the TBI group of Jackson. Once a month, we met to discuss any issues the clients had and often heard a speaker who presented news or information that pertained to Tennessee's brain-injured citizens. Here, we met Bobby and his mom, Kate, who were regular members of the group.

I remembered the year Bobby drove his car up an embankment that resulted in his brain injury. When we came to the first meeting, he smiled and hugged me. He even remembered that I had taught him in school and what we read. As with most brain-injured people, his long-term memory was excellent.

We also met Rebecca, who experienced two separate car accidents, both resulting in significant brain injuries. Her mother and I often discussed ways we could help brain-injured people in our area. We even took field trips to Jackson, Mississippi; Memphis; and Nashville to tour nonprofit organizations that housed brain-injured people and provided work for them. Most of these institutions housed not only brain-injured people, but people with other disabilities as well.

We felt we needed a place for brain-injured people in the Jackson area as their needs were very different from mentally disabled people's needs, mainly because the mentally disabled had no long-term memories. We began dreaming about creating such a place for our children and for children in West Tennessee who suffered from TBI.

We started by getting together with members from our immediate brain injury group once a month. We always had an art project for them to accomplish, such as tie-dyeing T-shirts, painting canvases, or making cement leaves. We planned to make enough items to have a TBI sale and fundraisers.

Over the next year, Joan bought a small house where we worked on weekends. The youth from First Presbyterian came often to work with us and help us create art projects. They also worked on the yard and planted rosebushes. After countless fundraisers, art projects, and sales, we made quite a bit of money, although not enough to begin building housing for our clients.

We held fundraisers at my friends' greenhouse, at the Old Country Store, and at Art in the Village. Ethel and Bud sponsored a skeet shoot for Bud's colleagues in West Tennessee. We went to local art sales and to West Tennessee AgResearch and Education Center. In addition, we held yard sales and sold items. Carriage House Antique Market and Cafe's owner gave us a space in the antique mall where we placed our handmade items to sell. We worked and worked, but what we needed was a sponsor or two. We explored every possible avenue but could not get a long-term commitment from anyone.

A member of my church gave us land on which we could build. Another person offered to buy us a van outright. Yet another promised to provide building materials. We will forever be grateful for these generous people. In the end, the people we contacted felt that our group was not large enough to warrant the long-term financial commitment our dream required.

Our dreams were dashed; our children would have to rely on relatives or institutions to provide for them once we were gone. Despite failing to accomplish our original plan, we did succeed in other ways. First, we provided an outlet for people with TBIs to get out and work their brains every weekend. Second, we broadcast information about the problems that brain-injured people faced in the community. Third, I would be remiss in saying that our efforts did not help me in my grieving process. I had to do something for Barry's future that would free Ben to live his life as he chose. When we finally closed the doors to Day by Day, our center's name, I was saddened but realized I would have to find another way.

We are now in a holding/healing pattern. We grieve, but we are moving out of the depths of suffering and pain on most days. In 1969, Elizabeth-Kubler Ross wrote *On Death and Dying*, a rather non-scientific account of how people grieve. She claims there are five stages of grief: denial, anger, bargaining, depression, and acceptance. I see that all the stages play a part in grieving, but my experience indicates that there are many other stages of mourning. The order in which the stages appear to someone in the grieving process varies as much as the people undergoing grief.

I cannot foresee a day for the rest of my life that I will not spend some time grieving: grieving the loss of Brad; grieving that Barry is not the same Barry we once had; grieving that Ben feels he needs to protect us; and grieving that Brian and I will not be grandparents.

At this point, we have adjusted to a new reality, but we live with the knowledge that the new reality is not permanent because time changes what happens in life. I have become more skillful in living day by day now than I ever was in my younger days.

My prayer now is more a prayer of thankfulness. If I ask for anything, I ask for strength, courage, resiliency, endurance, grace, and for God's presence to guide us.

Chapter 22

Telling the Bees

The human specialty seems to be brokenness—whether it be self-inflicted or brought about by fate. Feeling broken, feeling fractured, feeling that parts are missing, and feeling that we can't go on without being repaired is our condition. In order to go on, something within us has to happen; a metamorphosis must occur.

How does one arrive at the point where we are willing to live in a new norm? In this book, I have attempted to show how I have reinvented my life wheel over and over.

Mrs. Heller, whom I met in the year 2000, taught me about living life no matter the circumstances because it is our duty to live the life we were given in the best way we know and to teach others about the human condition. In 2000, the Tennessee Holocaust Commission presented me with the Belz-Lipman

Holocaust Educator of the Year Award for West Tennessee. I was truly honored to receive this award at The Peabody Hotel in the presence of approximately fifty survivors of the Holocaust.

The dedication on my award certificate reads:

> For us to speak with the young becomes ever more difficult. We see it as a duty and, at the same time, as a risk: the risk of appearing anachronistic, of not being listened to. We must be listened to. Above and beyond our personal experiences, we have collectively witnessed a fundamental, unexpected event, fundamental precisely because unexpected, not foreseen by anyone. It took place in the teeth of all forecasts; it happened in Europe; incredibly, it happened that an entire civilized people, just issued from the fervid flowering of the Weimar, followed a buffoon whose figure today inspires laughter, and yet Adolf Hitler was obeyed and his praises sung right up to catastrophe. It happened, therefore, it can happen again: This is the core of what we have to say.
> —Primo Levi, *The Drowned and the Saved*, 1986

More than the award, I was given an opportunity to visit with Mrs. Heller over a cup of coffee in the opulent setting of The Peabody, where we discussed the most horrific time in her life. She began her story after her liberation from Auschwitz. From there, she was sent to a hospital in France, where her emaciated, bruised, and broken body was expected to recuperate.

One day, when she was strong enough, she spied a scalpel carelessly left behind on one of the metal stands near her bed. With all her strength, she took the scalpel and cut out the tattooed number on her forearm. She wanted to remove any physical reminder of the hell in which she had lived. Unfortunately, she was never able to excise the horror of the concentration camp from her mind.

There were no tears in her eyes, only a faraway look that I realized took her back to Auschwitz. We were silent for a while as we sipped our coffees. Then, Mrs. Heller pulled her pink pullover up to her elbow and showed me the horrible scar that was created so long ago on her wrinkled forearm.

"I would have hundreds of these if I could just forget," she said. "But forgetting is not the answer for humanity. I need to remember so that as long as I live, I can be a testament to the horror."

I think of this as "the horror, the horror" that Joseph Conrad described in *The Heart of Darkness*: the horror of which man is capable.

I asked Mrs. Heller how she managed to continue with her life after experiencing so much excruciating pain when she had done nothing to deserve it.

"That is a question for which I have no answer," she said, adding softly, "I have asked God countless times why my family and I and my friends and others had to suffer and die."

"Why would He create a world in which suffering and life are synonymous?" she asked. "Maybe God has no answer for what His creations do to each other."

Later, Mrs. Heller married another survivor who passed away a few years ago. They had a daughter who was married. For the rest of the time we spent together, we talked about how important teachers were because they told the history of the Jews' and others' pain and suffering for inexplicable reasons.

"As long as I continue to teach, I will teach the history, the human suffering, of the Holocaust in my curriculum," I promised her.

Even though I had no part in the Holocaust, I do suffer from *Schadenfreude*, a German term that means the relief we feel when something bad happens to someone else instead of us. For the rest of my time with these Holocaust survivors, I felt something between anger, *Schadenfreude*, and resolve. Tim O'Brien writes in *The Things They Carried*:

> A true war story is never moral. It does not instruct, nor encourage virtue, nor suggest models of proper human behavior, nor restrain men from doing things men have done always. If a story seems moral, don't believe it. If at the end of a war story you feel uplifted, or if you feel some small bit of rectitude has been salvaged from the larger waste, then you have been made the victim of a very old and terrible lie. There is no rectitude whatsoever. There is no virtue. As a first rule of thumb, therefore, you can tell a true war story by its absolute and uncompromising allegiance to obscenity and evil.

So I have resolved to tell about the Holocaust without excuses and without sugarcoating a time in history that hurt and killed so many.

In *Night*, Elie Wiesel says, "To forget the dead would be akin to killing them a second time." I will take his quote even further and say that it is our duty to remember and tell our stories to others. Perhaps, something of our story will help another understand his own story. Writing our stories in books has become the modern way of "telling the bees" our troubles and pain.

Brian and I have found another way of "telling the bees." We tell the daylilies he grows. Brian tends to more than five hundred different daylilies with names such as 'Hold Your Horses,' 'Red Volunteer,' 'Moonlit Masquerade,' and 'Moses' Fire.' My favorite is a small, dark burgundy flower called 'Ed Murray.' Our joy every June is to walk among Brian's gardens and, yes, speak to the lovely blooms as they daily perform their colorful dance. Their remarkable beauty teaches an important lesson: Our job is to bring some beauty, some joy into our broken, unkind world each day.

As I walk among the blooms, I understand our personal lives much better. I know of only two ways to survive this world: Find God and speak to Him often, and try as best you can to take on life as it unfolds, day by day, as do the daylily blooms. We have taken their lessons to heart.

About the Author

Barbara Fowler graduated from Syracuse University and earned her master's degree from the University of Buffalo. She has taught for forty-four years in several middle schools, high schools, and colleges. Primarily, she taught German and English. In Jackson, Tennessee, she first taught at the Episcopal Day School, followed by the University School of Jackson, then at Tigrett Middle  School, and finally at Madison Academic Magnet High School. She also taught night classes at Union University in Jackson.

Barbara led many student groups to Europe and in the United States. She felt it was part of her job to open the world to her students. Trips included East and West Germany, Austria, Switzerland, Liechtenstein, Denmark, Italy, Greece, France, and England. In the US, students saw Mark Twain's Hannibal, Missouri; Washington, DC; and Pennsylvania. Students' worldview often changed because of their experiences on these trips, and that was Barbara's goal.

During her career, Barbara received several awards, including Teacher of the Year, Belz-Lipman Holocaust Teacher of the Year, and Tennis Coach of the Year. She also co-led Madison's Academic Decathlon teams to win first place in the nation for over ten years.

Since her retirement, Barbara has spent her time in her garden tending to more than five hundred varieties of daylilies. She also creates beautiful needlepoint pieces and writes when the spirit moves her. In addition, she is active with First Presbyterian Church's Service Committee, where she volunteers in various programs, including Gratitude Baskets and Meals on Wheels.

Barbara lives with her husband, Brian, and her children, Barry and Benjamin, in Jackson, Tennessee.

www.ingramcontent.com/pod-product-compliance
Lightning Source LLC
Chambersburg PA
CBHW051622120626
46551CB00014B/1908